Reaching the Summit

Avoiding & Reversing Decline in the Church

Across North America you can find churches that are on the edge. They are not always on the cutting edge and unfortunately not on the edge of breakthrough. They are finding themselves on the edge of *decline*. George Yates has provided a "heads-up" for the church of today in his book *Reaching the Summit*. Here is a book that guides church leaders through honest evaluation to determine where they are and where they are headed.

You are not without hope. The book prescribes critical keys for reversing course and leading the church into a healthy and thriving future. This book is not just for the struggling leader. Read it from wherever you are in your leadership journey to keep your congregation away from the edge of faltering and on a firm foundation of health.

—Dr. Steve R. Parr
Author of *Sunday School That Really Works* and *Sunday School That Really Responds*

To see what others are saying, see pages 141-143.

Reaching the Summit

AVOIDING AND REVERSING DECLINE IN THE CHURCH

GEORGE L. YATES

Essence PUBLISHING

Belleville, Ontario, Canada

REACHING THE SUMMIT
Copyright © 2012, George L. Yates

Scripture taken from the Holman Christian Standard Bible ® Copyright © 2003, 2002, 2000, 1999 by Holman Bible Publishers. All rights reserved. • Scripture taken from the HOLY BIBLE, NEW INTERNATIONAL VERSION ®. Copyright © 1973, 1978, 1984 by International Bible Society. Used by permission of Zondervan Publishing House. All rights reserved. • Scripture taken from *The Holy Bible, King James Version.* Copyright © 1977, 1984, Thomas Nelson Inc., Publishers.

ISBN: 978-1-55452-825-7
LSI Edition: 978-1-55452-826-4
E-book ISBN: 978-1-55452-827-1

Cataloguing data available from Library and Archives Canada

To order additional copies, visit:
www.essencebookstore.com

For more information, please contact:
SonC.A.R.E. Ministries
www.soncare.net
glyates@soncare.net

Essence Publishing is a Christian Book Publisher dedicated to furthering the work of Christ through the written word.
For more information, contact:
20 Hanna Court, Belleville, Ontario, Canada K8P 5J2.
Phone: 1-800-238-6376. Fax: (613) 962-3055.
Email: info@essence-publishing.com
Web site: www.essence-publishing.com

Contents

Foreword: Do You Want to Get Well?
John 5:1–10 NIV

Desperation marked all of their faces—hundreds of them—as they watched Him approach. Life and circumstances had not been kind to them. They were the blind, the lame, the disabled. And yet these people found in John 5 were about to have their lives changed.

As Jesus approached, He fixed His eyes on a man who could not walk. And upon learning that the man had been in this condition for thirty-eight years, Jesus asked a simple question. This question was so strikingly obvious that it was almost never asked. The question was this: *"Do you want to get well?"*

Do you want to get well? The paralyzed man did not answer this direct question. Instead he shared why he could not get well: *"Sir, I have no one to help me into the pool when the water is stirred. While I am trying to get in, someone else goes down ahead of me."* It was, perhaps, an excuse. *If only circumstances were different, if only he had family to help, if only others gave him some consideration, if only...*

To speak of illness requires little effort, planning, or sacrifice. To cure illness is another matter. A pastor of a dying church shared that he knew he should retire, but he needed the money, as his wife was very ill and her medications were expensive. Her illness was obvious. His spiritual illness was preventing him from trusting God to provide a path to save both his wife and the church. He had fallen lame in the land of faith.

Jesus did not comment about the lame man's response. He did not offer one word about how unfair life had been. Instead He changed the focus from why the paralyzed man could not be well to a test of his faith. It was a solitary test, depending on no outside circumstance. Cutting through all of the reasons and excuses, Jesus challenged this man to believe and obey: *"Get up! Pick up your mat and walk."*

The plight of the paralyzed man illustrates the dilemma we all face in ministry. We can talk about why we cannot be well, or we can obey Jesus and carry our ministry into the walking world of hope and progress.

As you read this book I pray that Jesus will appear in your thoughts and prayers and ask you, "Do you want to be well?" The test will be not in what you say but in what you are willing to do to become a ministry that rises to live again in the land of faith and obedience.

This book is dangerous in the hands of a ministry leader who believes that the church can be more than a weekly religious event. It describes the symptoms of the ailing church and gives sound ministry counsel as to finding the cure. The risk is in revealing the honest congregational answer to the question Jesus posed long ago, "Do you want to be well?'" I have personally observed George wisely coaching churches to confront their realities and move towards their dreams. The church has never had a better friend!

—Dr. Michael Stewart
Director of Missions, Central Coast Baptist Association

Acknowledgments

A sincere and heartfelt thank-you to all who helped make this book possible. First and foremost to my God and my Savior Jesus Christ, who considered me worthy through the shed blood of Christ to be used by Him.

To Dr. Michael Stewart, my friend and co-laborer in Christ, for your inspiration and idea that became the foreword.

To all those who read, reviewed, and so graciously endorsed this work before it was published.

To Susan Simpson, for your hours of diligent work in editing the original manuscript.

To Sherrill Brunton, my publishing manager; Tim Fransky, project editor; and the editing, creation, and printing teams at Essence Publishing. What a wonderful crew to work with.

To all the churches who have taught me so much in the field of ministry and brought me along on my journey while serving you.

To the most significant person in my life, my wife. Pam, you are truly God's gift to me. You are my support, my help, my encourager. Once again you have given more than anyone to see this work through. I love you dearly and am exceedingly grateful to have you by my side on this journey called life.

Thank You, Father. May You use this, Your work, to change perspectives, lives, and churches for years to come.

Introduction:
Examining the Causes of Decline

More churches in North America today are declining than are growing. Ed Stetzer, President of Lifeway Research, says that 80 percent of churches in North America today are stagnated or in decline.[1] Why are so many churches in decline today? What causes decline in churches?

If only it were simple to give you a one-sentence answer to those two questions. But it is not simple. In the following chapters we will attempt to answer not only these two questions; we will also give principles and ideas for avoiding and reversing decline in the church.

First, let me give my view of what constitutes a declining church. If in the current year a church has not added to its membership, attendance, or baptisms, it could be a declining church. If this trend continues for three years, I would definitely consider this a declining church. Also, if a church has not sent people out to start a new work and is only maintaining current members and ministry without signs of growth, it is likely a declining church.

Many churches look at their numbers and report, "We have not grown, but we have not lost either. We are still the same." The assumption is that these churches are not in decline. My assessment is that these churches *are* in decline and possibly in denial of decline. The good notice is that churches that are running the same in attendance as previous years are probably adding a few to their membership and attendance. But they are likely losing as many as they are adding. This attrition is due to people moving out of the area, dropping out of church attendance, or dying. To stay even in attendance, we must battle by adding 5 to 10 percent each year.

I believe there is more than one cause for decline, and each church has its own causes. Some churches face decline due to apathy within the church. Others suffer from decline because of a lack or loss of vision and purpose. Speaking with church members and leaders, you will find a plethora of reasons for the decline in churches today. However, most reasons can be traced back to one or possibly two causes.

If I had to list but one cause of decline in churches, I would reach for the words of Jesus to the church in Ephesus in Revelation 2:4: *"Yet I hold this against you: You have forsaken your first love"* (NIV).

I am not writing to condemn the church or church practices but to encourage and to uplift the church. This verse of Scripture is difficult for us to hear and accept about our own church. But we shouldn't stop reading at this verse alone. In the next verse Jesus gave us the cure. He said, *"Remember the height from which you have fallen! Repent and do the things you did at first"* (Revelation 2:5 NIV). What a glorious revelation from our Lord and Savior to the people of the church at Ephesus and to you and me as part of today's Church!

Churches do not intentionally walk away from their purpose (first love). Decline is certainly not in the motives or objectives of any church. Oftentimes we get caught up in the busyness of church life to the detriment of being the Church. Other times it is being the Church that begins the slide. Let's look at the two sides of this coin.

On the one hand, churches fall into decline due to the busyness of doing, instead of being, the Church. This happens when programs, events, and bureaucracy (administration) overtake spiritual preparation and ministry to the community. While the Church was theoretically designed to be self-feeding for spiritual growth, it was also instituted by God to feed the spiritual needs of the community. Therefore, we could say the Church is a twofold feeding station. It is 1) to feed spiritually and grow the members and regular attendees and 2) to reach out to meet the needs of the community, guiding them in spiritual matters and decisions as well.

The presumed need to keep programs and events going can overtake our passion and desire to serve God in reaching the lost communities around us. While this is never intentional, it is quite common in today's Christian culture in North America, especially in established churches that have been in existence for at least thirty years.

Because certain programs and events started as good and viable, our tendency is to keep them going as in previous eras. However, times change, the culture changes, and people change. A ministry event that worked well five years ago is likely not going to bring the same results today, especially if the ministry has not been evaluated, revised, and updated annually. This is how churches fall into the tradition mode, and following tradition for the sake of tradition will lead us straight to decline and extinction.

The second side of our coin is that sometimes "being the Church" begins the slide into decline. By the term *being the Church* I am referring to actually doing ministry as Jesus has called us to do. How can doing the "right stuff" lead to decline? Overreaching, taking on too much or too many ministry efforts, can plunge a church or other organization into decline. We might refer to this as the Rubbermaid concept.

In his writings, Jim Collins relates the story of the downfall of Rubbermaid, a longstanding Fortune 500 company. After decades of being the top in their industry, executives at Rubbermaid set in place larger than life goals. One particular goal was to produce at least one new product every day for the ensuing five years (365 days a year, 1,825 new products over five years). What a daunting undertaking! In addition the company's resolve was to enter at least one new area of business every twelve months. While there are many factors to any organization's decline, before the end of the five years of Rubbermaid's plan the debt load for the research and development of these lofty goals had the company slashing product lines and drastically cutting the work force and eventually selling out to another company for mere pennies on the dollar. The historic company—Rubbermaid—ceased to exist. What appeared at first as very lofty and aspiring goals led to the plummeting decline and extinction of the company.[2]

Church leaders can find themselves in a good and growing position and unwisely leap into more and more growth strategies and ministries at the neglect of the passion that brought the initial achievement. This will often lead to decline by way of exhaustion, stretching resources and people too thin, and burnout.

It is imperative that church and ministry leaders make an objective evaluation of the reality of all aspects and facts of their ministry setting. I suggest that the best way to conduct a truly objective evaluation of all the facts is to bring in a neutral observer from outside the ministry or church. This should be someone such as a seasoned consultant, coach, or strategist, trained and experienced in asking probing questions that the church leaders and members might not think of or want to bring to the table on their own.

There is a growing ministry today of Christian coaching, and this can be very valuable to churches and individuals in sustaining health and growth. A coach is one who is trained in bringing out of the players (church leaders and members) what is otherwise hidden and covered up. A coach is not a mentor, though mentoring might become part of the coaching process. A coach is not a consultant, though consulting will be part of the process. A coach is a person who has the ability to see the big picture of your ministry from a vantage point you do not have. Upon seeing from this vantage point, a coach is equipped to formulate questions that allow you to explore the unknown or unused wisdom, experience, and discernment of your ministry and the members of your church or organization.

A word of caution is in order here: be very careful when choosing a coach. I suggest you seek out a Christian coach who has experience in the church setting. You want to find one who has experience in growing and maintaining healthy ministry and one who knows how to properly formulate the needed questions while facilitating a healthy forward-moving process of reversing decline. You are not looking for someone who only wants to give suggestions but for an experienced coach who is willing to walk with you through the process and who knows and relates to your doctrinal positions.

In making an objective evaluation of your ministry setting, begin with these two questions:

1) What happened leading up to the point at which decline became visible?
2) What did the organization do in the wake of this visible evidence?

The answer to the first question most often has to do with a financial shortage or a loss of key lay leaders in the church. Until there is a shortage of financial resources or manpower to carry out ministry, many church leaders ignore the signs of decline.

The second question is designed to allow church leaders to review actions taken or the lack of action. While it is designed in an attempt to keep leaders from moving to defensive responses, some will instinctively react with a defensive reply.

A coach might ask additional questions to assist in understanding the motives and actions of the church, enabling him to assist church leaders in recognizing any misguided actions as well as good achievements.

Churches that have been in decline for several years have a tendency to gradually move to what I refer to as a turned-in mentality (not reaching or benefiting the community). One line of questioning I have used at times is to ask for the thoughts of church members and leaders on the strengths of the church. (What is the church good at doing?) I have a scribe write on a board or large sheet of paper all of the responses. After everyone has had a chance to list his or her ideas of the strengths of the church, we take each response one by one and ask the question, "Who is this for?" When someone responds I ask, "Is that someone in the community or church members?"

Normally the trend is that most, if not all, of the perceived strengths in a declining church are for the church members, not the community or the lost world. Sometimes it takes two or three questions to bring the realization to the table.

For example, one response at a particular church was "We prepare and carry meals to senior shut-ins."

"Who are these shut-ins?"

"People who can't get out." (As if I didn't know this already.)

"How do you get the names of these shut-ins?"

"We know them."

"How do you know them?"

"They are members of our church or their family comes here."

The realization was that this might have been a strength of the church, but it was not being used as an outreach or strength to grow the church. It was "for members only." I then led these church members in discussion using a series of questions to help them see how, if this was a strength of the church, it could be used to carry the love of God to other shut-ins outside the church.

Most churches in decline have strengths that could be used in reaching the lost, but they have forgotten and drifted toward a turned-in ministry—turned in to only the members of the church.

Leaders of a declining organization must come to the realization that the organization is in decline and that their actions (or inactions) may have contributed to the cause of the decline. However, it is not necessarily time to throw in the towel. There are principles and steps to reverse the trend of decline. There must be a "want to" attitude among the leaders first and also among the members of the organization. We will look at this closer in the steps to reversing decline. However, first it would be wise to look at the phases of decline.

Before you read further in this book, stop and pray, asking God to open your heart to see and realize the need in your own church to ensure avoidance or reversal of declining trends. Pray that you would read each word seeking to rekindle the flame and your passion for growing a healthy church (body of believers) for God's glory and His kingdom. May God bless and grow you through your reading and implementing of principles and practices found in the following pages.

Section One

The Phases of Decline

Recently, while I was returning home from a speaking engagement, the airplane I was on was experiencing turbulence as we began descending toward our destination. I fly quite regularly, so I am used to turbulence, and I have experienced harsher turbulence than on this particular flight. However, there was something new to me with this experience.

It was late at night, so it was dark in the cabin as well as outside. As we descended through the blackness of night and thunderstorm clouds, bouncing with the turbulence, suddenly the plane dropped. The drop was so sudden and significant that it lifted everyone out of our seats. The incident only lasted for a second or perhaps a second and a half. I'm not certain how far we dropped, probably only a few feet. I believe I do not want to know how far it actually was. The pilot was masterful and got us to our destination safe and on time.

Most organizations do not fall in one clear-cut knock-down drop. There is normally a series of digressions. An examination of the organization will, in most cases, show a departure from the original purpose and core values of the organization. The initial signs of decline may be subtle and ignored or explained away. This first phase can go on for several years without notice.

In the church, for example, early decline in attendance is most always excused as "We had several families move away" or "Several of our members passed away, and their families no longer attend." Another familiar line is "Our senior adults just can't get out like they once could." A decline in financial support is often explained away with statements involving the economy or loss of jobs in the community.

In these statements and most others given, the reasons are outward focused. All of the reasons (or excuses) have to do with outside influences that we have little or no control over, because it is easier and less painful to excuse decline as the fault of someone or something else than to accept responsibility for something we did or did not do. Rarely is thought given to the possibility of impact from the organization's leadership or ministry practices. We do not want to look inside.

When I was a child, everyone liked playing "Pin the tail on the donkey." But no one wanted to be the donkey. One does not take favorably to "pinning" something on oneself or allowing others to pin something on us. Whether we want to admit it or not, organizational decline is most often self-inflicted.

I believe there are phases of decline that a church or similar organization encounters. While the first two phases are normally subtle and slow at producing decline, they are critical, as the years a church lives in phase 1 and 2 are pouring a new false foundation for the church. This false foundation is one of indifference and disconcerting mind-sets for church members and leaders alike. If this is not addressed and a course set for reversal, it will lead to an apathetic viewpoint of the unchurched souls of your community and beyond. Furthermore, it will catapult you into deeper decline.

Once this mind-set establishes itself, the self-infliction of decline increases, and the further into decline a church recesses, the more in-turned the church becomes. *In-turned* means we become less and less outward focused and more and more content with doing things for the members inside the church at the expense of the lost communities we have been called to serve. The purpose or mission moves from reaching the lost for Christ to "We're here; we hope you come" to "If they come, they come; if not, it is their fault" to "Why aren't we growing? They won't come" to "I just don't know what happened. We tried." Organizational decline is in most cases self-inflicted. And oftentimes we do not even realize it.

The good news is that a church can make a turnaround and experience reversal of declining trends in any of the first four phases of decline. The further into decline a church sinks without seeking help to "dig out" and reverse declining trends, the more difficulty it will experience. Certainly the further into decline one drops, the more work will be involved to eradicate and reverse the trends of decline. But isn't restoring God's work for His purposes truly worth the effort?

We will discuss the five phases of decline in this writing as follows:

Phase 1: Loss of Vision
Phase 2: Lack of Purpose
Phase 3: Denial
Phase 4: Grasping for Survival
Phase 5: Relinquishment of Ministry

I encourage you when reading this material to not skip any chapter or phase you think might not apply to your church. It is important to read each chapter about the phases to truly understand how they build on each other and for a full realization of where your church is and where it might be headed. Every church at some point will enter phase 1 of decline. How quickly you realize the phase of decline your church is in and how soon you act to reverse the decline will determine the success and future of the church.

Unfortunately, in many churches the climb back from phase 4 becomes too arduous and too steep of a climb for the lingering remnant of the church. It is time to relinquish the ministry of this community to someone else. In some cases a new and fresh approach by a different group may be successful at revitalizing God's ministry to the community. Before your church reaches phase 5, let's read on and find the way back to fulfilling God's purpose for your church as you reach for the summit of your ministry.

1

Phase 1: Loss of Vision

Phase 1 of decline often goes unnoticed by church members and, in most scenarios, even by the leaders of the church. This is because phase 1 of decline is most always very subtle, the most subtle of all phases. Phase 1 goes undetected because it is the loss of a family here, a member there, a young couple moving away for better job opportunities, and the death of one or two senior adults. Phase 1 goes undetected as decline because it is one member or family at a time, and no correlation is recognized. We accept it as part of life in our society and culture today.

Early stages of decline are often explained away using statements such as those listed in the introduction to this section, "The Phases of Decline," with little or no concern that decline will continue. At this stage there is no stopguard put in place. Very few churches while in phase 1 of decline will attempt to examine decline or begin a strategy planning process to protect against further decline.

George Bullard says a church oftentimes enters this stage "simply by relaxing and taking a breath as an organism following a generation of hard work."[3] With any organization it is a common fallacy to assume that when things are going well with several years of prosperity behind us, things will continue to go well.

Through the early years of slow but steady decline, churches will drift farther from their sense of vision and purpose. It is not an intentional drift. It is much like a vacationer on an inflatable raft floating at the ocean's beach who allows the warmth of the sun and the gentle rocking of the waves to lull him into a state somewhere between awareness and sleep. It doesn't take long for the ocean's current to pull the vacationer several hundred yards from his starting point. He awakens to unfamiliar surroundings. In some cases the vacationer has been pulled out to sea without knowing and must be rescued.

In the church it is not an intentional drift, but somewhere along the way we have let the warmth of ministry and the gentle rocking of weekly gatherings with friends lull us into that state of being somewhere between spiritual awareness and sleep. For some, perhaps we have been lulled into a deep sleep.

An observation in several churches has been that in following the achievement of the initial vision, a couple of things happen. One of the greatest detriments is the leadership not recasting the vision. In the early 1990s, I was in a meeting with several leaders of a church one evening. The church was founded in the early 1960s and now found itself at a crossroads. The church had reached capacity on Sundays, and growth was being stifled. There was little or no classroom space available for new classes, they had two worship services, and additional parking was needed.

Several ideas were brought up at the meeting, including buying adjacent property and building something new or buying new property and moving. There was one statement made that evening that will forever ring in my mind. One of the elder members, who had been a member since the early days of the church, stated, "When we moved here we laid out what we would build here (over time), and that was all we would build. This building we are sitting in was the last of those buildings."

At that moment my eyes probably grew to about three times their normal size and my mouth dropped to my knees. It was easy to read the faces of the men in the room. Several of the men (longer term members) were, at that instant, resigned to status quo. What that man said in essence was "We had a vision. We accomplished the vision. There has been no vision cast since." I am not certain if that is what he meant or not. But that is what I and the others in the room heard that night.

Fortunately, the church was willing to accept a new vision and move forward. God blessed the church greatly. They continued to grow and are now in a new and beautiful facility with many offerings for community ministry. Unfortunately, in other churches a similar statement would have carried the day and caused further decline in membership, attendance, and the growth of God's kingdom, ultimately leading to the death of the church.

One of the imperatives in my mind is that the vision for an organization must continually be kept in front of the people of the organization. The light of the vision must be kept burning bright and must be updated and recast from time to time. By recasting the vision we are not saying change the vision by throwing out the old and starting over. No, you recast the vision by celebrating the victories of accomplished vision and stretching the vision further into the future. The following is a simplified example:

"In the following month we will be celebrating the achievement of stage 1 of our vision. We are so grateful to each of you and to God using you to surpass this milestone. And as we celebrate we want to continue to look to the future. We still have stage 2 and 3 to accomplish. We are in stage 2, and God is blessing. I want to encourage you to continue pressing on until we complete stage 2 and move into stage 3. I also want to share with you something very exciting, and that is what we are referring to as the next stage of our vision. God is so gracious."

While reading the last paragraph, perhaps you got excited and wanted to hear what stage 4 was. The idea is to build continued excitement in everyone involved by sharing and recasting the vision. After all, if it is God's vision, shouldn't we be excited about it? When you share the excitement, God will build in the motivation.

The longer a church goes without a renewed vision, the further it will plunge into decline. Without a strong renewed vision, the church or organization will drift away from its stated purpose. Churches are started because a group of people have a passion and a burden to share God's love and His Word with a community or people group. Without a strong vision, the desire for fulfilling the purpose vanishes.

Proverbs 29:18 says, "*Where there is no vision, the people perish*" (KJV). I like to say, "Where there is no vision, the people will leave your parish." People need a cause, a mental picture of something to work toward. In contrast to some beliefs, people really do want expectations. A clear, concise vision that members can take ownership of will bring about the desire to execute expectations leading to the fulfillment of the organization's purpose and vision. A vision must be clear and succinct for members to grasp and carry out the vision.

Not only must it be clear and succinct, but a vision must be articulated in various forms and communicated frequently through assorted forms of communication and in various settings. The vision must be kept in front of the people of the church at every level and function of the church.

The church should hear it frequently from the pastor in the pulpit and from the staff in smaller group settings.

The vision should be in print in the bulletin, church newsletter, and other publications. A word of caution; do not use the same wording in each printing of the vision. Change it up; give some examples of how the church is attempting to fulfill the vision. Share brief written testimonies of victories of people serving to accomplish the vision.

The vision should appear on bulletin boards and posters throughout the church facilities.

You should be able to boil the vision down to ten words or less. Then you can use it on T-shirts and postcards or even business cards.

Find ways to use multimedia to communicate the vision. Put together video clips and photos of members undertaking to fulfill the vision. Incorporate multimedia into your worship service program.

In one church where I served, the music minister wrote a song about the vision of the church. The choir taught it to the congregation, and it was part of the worship service every week.

A printed version or photo with caption of the vision should appear on every page of the church Web site.

The list can go on and on. The main imperative here is to keep in front of the people of the church the vision of what the church is attempting to accomplish for God through the power of God.

In casting the vision, church leaders must provide opportunities and training in how to share and serve God through the vision. Talk is talk, and the flesh is the flesh. You can cast a great vision using the finest and flashiest of modern technology, but if you do not provide concrete opportunities to serve, will you be anything more than a sounding gong or a clanging cymbal?

Few people will get out and work for your vision on their own impetus. People need opportunities provided for them to serve in fulfilling the mental picture you have painted of the vision for kingdom work. Regular vision emphasis through your ongoing biblical teaching strategies and programs is critical to growing your members into ministry-active believers.

With a renewed vision that is kept in front of them, church members will be more likely to continue to strive and serve the church and its ministries as an outward reaching organism with a renewed passion for serving God. Church leadership championing the vision and celebrating even the smallest of victories with the congregation will lead greatly to avoiding or reversing decline in your church, even before decline is recognized.

2

Phase 2: Lack of Purpose

The next phase of decline can be realized in a church when the decline begins to affect the ministry of the church. Two of the greatest areas to notice in this phase are

1) when the attendance or membership decline reaches a point where replacing capable leadership becomes difficult and ministries and programs begin to be compromised or condensed
2) when decreasing financial support initiates a strain on resourcing current ministry and staff

In the first scenario, when a church begins to lose some of its key leaders, often the remaining current leaders take on extra responsibility. As the church continues to decline and more leaders exit the church, some of these same leaders will take on yet another position of responsibility. And the cycle continues. It is not uncommon to see five to eight people in a smaller declining church (150 or fewer members) each carry five to seven areas of responsibility (and sometimes more).

One church I worked with faced this dilemma. This church was averaging about 125 in worship on Sunday morning. A few people in the church were carrying the major load of responsibilities for church administration and ministry. One woman served as treasurer, head of the kitchen, team leader for the church's evangelism program, part-time office volunteer, finance committee member, preschool worker, choir member, chair of the bereavement committee, cook for Wednesday evening meals, and on-rotation children's church worker. And these are just the ten that I can remember. Her husband was almost as busy at the church. If I remember correctly, he had seven positions of responsibility in the church.

This couple was not trying to take over the church. Rather, they had such a passion for the church that when a leadership position was open and no one stepped up to fill it, they were two of about five people who would step in and undertake the responsibility. God bless people like this who are willing servants with a passion! However, too often this leads to burnout and the loss of even these willing leaders. (Thankfully this did not happen to the couple aforementioned. They are still serving faithfully—in fewer positions now.)

Missed Opportunities

As I worked with the church, I recognized two missed opportunities. My first assumption was that this church had done very little if any leadership development in the previous ten years, which church members later affirmed to be true. If not building potential leaders and opening up to offer leadership responsibilities, the church will lose potential leaders. Thus began part of the church's decline.

Contrary to some belief, people do want expectations. Satisfaction comes from serving and leading. Churches need an open door to leadership development and a strategic process for seeking, recruiting, and developing new and future leaders.

The second missed opportunity I recognized in this church was that when things were going good, those who were in leadership positions remained in the positions until relocation due to retirement, job relocation, or death. There was nothing in place to train new leaders or give younger and newer members an opportunity to move into leadership positions. This was not a blatant closed-door policy of the church. It was simply an oversight.

Several years earlier, things were going okay for the church. Positions were filled; the programs and ministry were being carried out. These are all signs of phase 1 of decline, which the church had not realized. One good stop-guard for this scenario is to have a policy for every leader to be apprenticing a potential leader.

One thing that often occurs in small churches is that two or three people pass a position back and forth. One, let us say Mr. Smith, will serve in a position for a term as per the church bylaws. When his term is over, the position is passed to a second individual, Mrs. Davis. When Mrs. Davis's term is over, the position will go back to Mr. Smith. And the cycle continues.

Good——the Enemy of Great

The church being discussed had gone through phase 1 of decline without noticing it. And now that they were in phase 2, the personnel, the leadership of the church, was being affected. While these people were doing a good job at their respective responsibilities and keeping the church alive, good is always the enemy of great.

Our enemy, Satan, is not afraid of us attempting to be good. If our focus is on good, we cannot make the leap to greatness. The best efforts of success come out of greatness. Good is always the enemy of great. Superman is a myth. And not even Superman was great at all things. As Clark Kent he was not the greatest of communicators. Superman had his faults.

Too often we settle for good when God created us to be great in service to Him. No one can take on five, seven, or ten areas of responsibility in the church and perform to the best of his ability in any of the areas. It is physically impossible. Given the choice, I would rather have a person be great at one thing she is passionate about than have her attempt to be good at six things pulling at her time and talents from different directions.

Wounded Ministries

Because of the shortage of leaders in this phase, ministries begin to suffer as well. The initial response is to cut the ministry or to combine two ministries. Some of the first ministries cut will be those related to causes outside the church. The first to go will be the ones that bear a cost on the church budget. The outside ministries that remain will be only the ones that do not affect the church budget or have a champion inside the church—someone who will fight to keep the ministry effort alive.

There is another group of outside ministries that will be shut down during this phase. These are the ministries that require the most manpower. The truth is, these will most likely shut themselves down in the second phase of decline. They will shut themselves down because the church has been losing manpower for several years, and most likely there have been fewer and fewer people involved in these ministries during the years of decline. These ministries may continue in decline until there are no longer enough willing servants to carry out the ministries. Then they will be quietly and reverently shuffled off to the ministry cemetery.

Unchecked Control

In working with one church, I discovered that two men held "controlling" positions in the church and exchanged the positions at the end of each term. For example, one would chair the finance committee while the other chaired the personnel committee. When the term of service was completed, they simply switched positions. At the end of the next term, they switched back. These two gentlemen also held most every position in the church that would possibly make decisions or bring about change.

While I believe these two gentlemen were given positions of authority to help protect the church during a difficult period, what was intended for good carried into a bad situation for the church. The church had lost over 80 percent of its members, attendance, and revenues. Yet these men continued to carry on, each year having to accept more and more areas of responsibilities as others left the church. What began as a good and possibly right-for-the-moment decision had created a downward spiral that was not easily corrected. The church had fallen deep into phase 4 due to a decision made most likely in phase 2 of the decline of the church.

Decrease of Financial Support

The second scenario mentioned earlier is the decrease of financial support. With the decline of attendance and members comes the decline of financial support as well. When we have built a ministry on a projected budget and the financial support does not come in as expected, decisions must be made. Spending must be curtailed, and all areas of the budget need to be examined with certain scrutiny.

Every budget will have fixed categories. These are areas that you, as the church, have little or no control over, such as utilities, mortgages, insurance, etc. There are in most cases some of these areas where some "belt tightening" can be established, though as a general rule not a large amount can be cut from these budget items.

The largest portion of most church budgets is tied up in personnel costs: salaries, taxes, insurance, and other benefits. Since it is the largest portion, it is the first place some church members want to cut. While this at first may seem to be the most logical place to start, members need to think of what this means. I often ask churches considering this, "If this was the company you work for, would you be so quick to tell them to begin by looking at cutting your salary or terminating your employment?"

If personnel is cut, who will take on the extra responsibility? Churches have paid personnel because volunteers could not be found with the time, availability, or ability to carry out the responsibilities required. When personnel is cut in this manner, ministry will always suffer, and in most cases decline will continue. A church should ask itself, "Are we looking for a tourniquet, or do we desire to stop the bleeding and work toward a healing of the wound (to stop and reverse the declining trends)?"

Personnel may very well be one of the areas to look at, but consider the human being and the family represented in each line of the personnel section of the budget. We also must look at the ministry being performed. If this person is responsible for a fruitful part of the church ministry and producing valid church growth, a good hard look should be taken before dropping the axe.

Rather than going in and starting to cut people or salaries, the organization should look at what strategies can be put in place to first stop the bleeding, so to speak. Personnel could very well be that place, but use caution in proceeding. There are formulas churches can use as a guideline for personnel based on attendance and budget resources.

The next step would be to look for the excess in the budget. One of the first questions asked when looking at trimming the budget by cutting personnel should be "Do we have the right people in the right positions?" (See chapter 6, "Filling Positions With the Right People.")

Mistakes of Ministry Cuts

In most churches one of the first areas of budget to be cut involves ministry and missions. After all, this is what we consider to be discretionary budget areas—"We do not have to have it." We begin to cut funding for curriculum and ministry resources.

There is possibly some surplus that can be reduced in some of these areas. But is this not where we intend to "grow" Christians? In some churches total ministries are cut and wiped out, never to be carried out by the church again. The sad part of this is, while it is often the first area to be cut, it also is the smallest area of most church budgets to begin with, and it is the one area of budget most closely related to the original purpose of the church.

I encourage churches to evaluate every ministry each year. See appendix 1 for ministry evaluation. There are some ministries that may need to cease or to be curtailed for a season. There are certain ministries that run their course, and after a particular number of years they should be discarded. Then there are areas of ministry that should be evaluated but not discarded.

Two of these are Sunday school and small-group Bible study. Instead of being discarded, these vital ministries should be evaluated for effectiveness and for areas of needed improvement. What equipping, training, and outside counsel can you acquire to address these areas of greatly needed improvement?

Of course if these annual evaluations had been objectively carried out over the history of the church, it is very probable that the church would not be in the midst of phase 2 of decline.

Churches too often are afraid to go outside the church for assistance and training, for a couple of reasons. The first is a pride issue: "If we bring someone in, we are admitting we cannot do it on our own." Let me give you a newsflash: God never intended you to "do it" on your own. The second is, when a church is in decline, church leaders see bringing in outside assistance as an unnecessary cost. "Our budget is already stressed; we can't afford it." The reality is, *not* bringing someone in will most likely be more costly to the church's future and will lead you into further decline.

With phase 2 some church leaders become aware that there is reason for concern. The reaction in many churches at this point is to increase discipleship class offerings. While this is commendable, it is not in most cases a "fix" for the problem at hand. This continues the in-turning of the church. By in-turning, we are speaking of inward focused. In phase 2, churches may begin to react to decline in attendance by focusing on the remaining members, adding more discipleship classes and more events for the members of the church. The outward expression is "We are doing this to try to build up the church." However, the majority of emphasis is on "us," at the expense of the community around "us" and the original purpose of the church.

More classes and more committees do not automatically equal more ministry. Oftentimes it produces less ministry, in large part due to the amount of time today's members have for "church." When we increase the need for people to spend time in classes, committees, and meetings, we take away from their time to spend serving.

Each of these elements of phase 2 will lead a church into phase 3 of decline.

3

Phase 3: Denial of Reality

A church moves into phase 3 when the evidence of decline becomes obvious to those inside as well as outside the church. In this phase church leaders often enter a stage of denial. It is hard to ignore when church attendance drops from 300 to 200 or from 125 to 84. If Sears lost one-third of its customer base, someone in leadership would take notice. In an organization such as Sears, action would be taken long before this size loss occurred. Yet in some churches the realization of the denial phase may not happen until the church has lost up to half its attendance in an average week.

Jim Collins states, "There is a tendency to discount or explain away negative data rather than presume that something is wrong with the company (organization)."[4] In the church this is all too common. Church leaders are busy. With weekly services, visiting the sick and grieved, ministry programs, committee meetings, and sermon and teaching preparation, there is so much going on in the ministry of the church that it is hard to accept the data declaring decline.

Pass the Blame or Shoulder Responsibility

In the church one way we attempt to explain away the obvious data is to blame outside sources. It is much easier to pass the blame on to outside influences that we have no control over than it is to accept our role in the decline of the church. We need to accept responsibility for the ministry effort and the community to which God has called us. Great leaders shoulder the responsibility rather than passing the blame for decline in the church.

Though denial has actually been a characteristic of church leadership in phases 1 and 2, in phase 3 denial becomes apparent as some church leaders become vocal in rejecting the obvious. Denial becomes a pattern. This is a point where first the leaders, then the members of the organization, need to address the blunt reality and facts of the situation, what I refer to as having a vigorous face-to-face summit with reality (see chapter 7, "A Vigorous Face-to-Face Summit With Reality").

Unfortunately, we often see denial of the truth of the church's situation and a refusal to conduct an open and honest assessment of the ministry's decline. Instead, what we frequently see in the church is 1) changing what we count, and 2) an increased emphasis on doing more of what we have been doing and trying harder with our existing ministries and personnel (volunteer and paid staff).

Counting Practices

For some reason, leaders often think the way to correct the situation is to change the way we count or, more frequently, change what we count. In church as well as other areas of life, we count what is important to us, and what we count is what becomes important. So, do our values change when we change what we count? I'll let you come to your own conclusion.

Most churches have certain factors they keep track of on a continual basis. These articles (factors) that a church tracks or counts are supposedly a way of helping us compare how we are doing this year versus previous years. For years most churches have tracked or counted items such as people in attendance at services and events, new people who have joined the congregation over the past year, and how much money is brought in through member giving and similar observable items. Many churches track other items as well. However, changing the way a church counts is often a result of decline.

For instance, I know of churches that had always counted people in their Sunday morning worship. When facing noticeable decline, these churches changed the way they counted. Instead of counting only the people attending on Sunday morning, some began also counting those who were unable to attend but who would receive an audio copy of the service or a printed copy of the study curriculum. One predominantly Caucasian church that had a Spanish congregation meeting in their facility began recording the attendance of the two congregations as one. Now, I am not sitting in judgment on either of these or other congregations. Rather, I am merely stating some of the changes in "counting practices" that I have seen as a result of phase 3 decline in churches.

Ed Stetzer and Thom Rainer in their book *Transformational Church* take a look at "the scorecard," what we count, and suggest that a new and different scorecard is needed for the healthy and growing churches of the twenty-first century.[5] Stetzer and Rainer are not condoning changing what we count to make our numbers look good. What they are advocating is evaluating what we count and developing a scorecard that more closely validates forward-moving ministry, fulfilling the Great Commission.

Working Harder, Doing More

The second area of denial in this phase of decline in churches is an increased emphasis on doing more of what we have been doing and trying harder. For some reason, church leaders assume that attempting more of the same things we have been doing will bring different and better results. If you keep doing what you've always been doing, you are not going to get different results. Two plus two always equals four. To "do" more of the same things will only bring similar results and may drive you further into decline at a faster pace.

If I attempt to light my gas grill with the manufacturer's push button igniter and it will not light, there comes a point when I begin to look for the source of the problem. It may very well be that the igniter is worn out. I am not going to continue pushing the button right through mealtime, wondering when it will light. I will resort to a secondary lighting source (a match) or a different cooking method. In churches we keep pushing the igniter button, hoping it will eventually light the grill. More and more pushes on a device that is not working will not bring it back to life.

If your car does not start after several attempts, you will not sit in the driver's seat and continue cranking and cranking, attempting to start it. You will begin looking for potential problems, consult your owner's manual, or call someone who can help. Why do we not follow this same pattern in the Church? Instead, we continue attempting to crank a dead car in hopes of bringing it back to life.

41

In Western movies when a horse dies under its rider, how many times have you seen the rider stay on top of the dead horse and continue kicking at its flanks to keep going? You cannot ride a dead horse. You need an immediate dismount, or the horse will fall on you, perhaps pinning your leg and keeping you from continuing on. To reverse decline in a church or similar organization, you sometimes have to recognize the dead horses (ministries inside the church), dismount, and find a new mount (a new ministry meeting the needs of the community). What is going to carry you to the next level and reverse the decline?

I am not by any means saying replace everything you know and do as a church. But doing more and more of the same and expecting different results is not the answer. This will not reverse decline or rebuild your church. It will only take you further into decline.

Neither am I advocating that all pastors and leaders leave their churches. In fact, this has become detrimental to many churches, when leaders would rather jump ship and find a different church to try another attempt at success. In many cases, that pastor or leader will find a similar declining situation at his next church. And he will likely stay at this church until it reaches phase 3 and once again dismount for yet another church. This is not healthy for the pastor or any of his churches, though each church might experience a couple of years of small growth or plateau. We grow through the trials and adversity in our lives. If you want to grow in your spiritual leadership abilities, serve God through the trials and adversities. After all, the grass is not always greener on the other side of the fence.

I also believe there are times when a pastor or other staff person has overstayed his calling at a particular ministry.

Each staff person should always be vigilant about his or her contribution to the growth or decline of the church, God's calling on his or her life, and be willing to accept when it is time to move on. A good rule of thumb for paid staff or any church member: when you leave a church, be certain you are running *to* something and not running away. Stay true to God and His calling on your life, and He will lead you, even when you have been serving at a subpar level.

Perspective

Reversing decline in your church requires strategic planning following an examination of the cold, hard facts of where we have been, recent results, and needed changes (see chapter 7, "A Vigorous Face-to-Face Summit with Reality"). Reversing decline is not an overnight turnaround, but it can be accomplished. The longer decline is allowed to continue, the deeper into the phases of decline a church will plunge and the more determination and resolve the reversal will take.

Turning a deaf ear or a blind eye to the severity of reality will not bring about the needed changes that will reverse decline in the church. We must engage in a vigorous face-to-face summit with reality and continually refine the path to achieving the purpose of our church, fulfilling the Great Commission. You and your church will be much better off bringing in an experienced coach and consultant to assist you with the assessment of your ministry (vigorous face-to-face summit with reality).

An experienced outsider trained and equipped in asking the right questions will bring the objective perspective of reality to the table. Without this perspective, you have less of a chance to succeed in reversing the decline in your church. God has not given any one person all the answers or all the gifts needed to turn a church around. But your church leadership together with a trained, experienced person from outside your church can recognize the severity of the situation, and God's new direction can be found.

It is time to move from denial of what is happening and passing the blame to accepting responsibility and conducting a vigorous face-to-face summit with reality before your church drops further into the phases of decline.

4

Phase 4: Grasping for Survival

In the decline of every organization, there comes a time when the organization realizes that the methods, products, or systems of the past are not working and a staggering change is necessary, and the change needed to begin yesterday. The leadership in many organizations suddenly switches to survival mode. The ship is going down, and the first thought is to throw everything overboard that is weighing the ship down.

There may be extra, unneeded baggage on the ship, but first priority should go to determining the cause of the vessel's sinking. The ship is possibly going down because there is a hole in the hull below the waterline. If so, no matter what you cast off the boat, the hole will continue to fill with water.

In most scenarios, I see the casting overboard of items of weight as three things:

1) A knee-jerk reaction
2) A waste of time and manpower that could be used to diagnose and begin repairing the cause of sinking
3) Casting off some of the very items you will need to make repairs to stop the sinking

As in other businesses and organizations, the church is often guilty of looking for and focusing on symptoms instead of causes. My wife suffered from chronic back pain for several years. At one point it became severe and was interrupting her life, health, and well-being. For two years we drove the sixty-mile round trip to see her doctor, sometimes on a weekly basis.

It was during this time that I realized why a health maintenance organization (HMO) actually exists. The doctors kept telling Pam they were trying to help her manage the pain. To this she replied, "I do not want to manage the pain; I want to get rid of it." The doctors tried different types of therapy and management techniques the first few months, to no avail. Afterwards they began giving Pam injections of different medications.

Every four to six weeks Pam received another injection, something different from the last. Epidurals, blocks—everything was a mask, not a potential healer. The injections were mere attempts to mask the pain, to keep Pam from feeling the pain. One danger that I feared with these injections was that Pam could easily cause more damage to her back without knowing, from the few injections that actually did mask the pain.

When I asked a doctor why they were only treating symptoms and not trying to treat the cause or correct the damage, his reply to me was "That's not what we do here. We help you manage the pain." And this was one of the largest HMOs in the nation, the largest on the west coast. Our conversation carried on for a couple of minutes, though nothing changed—that is, nothing except our resolve.

We began researching, and a friend found a solution. We located a back surgeon who had changed his technique a few years earlier when he had back problems of his own. My wife had the surgery (for four bulging and herniated discs). There was no incision, only four puncture marks. All four discs were repaired. My wife has not had one minute of back pain since the surgery in 2006. She was cured, completely healed. We paid out of pocket for my wife to have the surgery since we went outside of our insurance (HMO). It was the best investment we ever made.

I share this story with you because church life often becomes much like the first set of doctors treating Pam's health issues with her back. We look for symptoms and think we can "fix" the problem by addressing the symptoms. Oftentimes, like the doctors, all we are doing is hiding the pain. The issue of decline is still with us.

For example, a church that realizes it has wandered away from reaching out to the community may react by offering more classes on evangelism and addressing the need through other means, messages, etc. The emphasis becomes more classes, not more outreach opportunities. While these may be helpful, little will change without providing the church members opportunities and practical applications to practice their ability and faith. We are only working to hide the pain of decline.

Grasping

This also becomes the grasping phase. As a church or similar organization sinks further in decline, it begins to grasp for that one silver bullet, that one great saving program or event or style change. Sinking deeply enough, some churches will grasp for anything that might still float.

In the mid 1990s, a pastor burst on the scene of evangelicals in America. Actually, he did not burst on the scene at that time. This was simply when his church became known to most of America. Rick Warren had been growing a church (people) for more than ten years—a church that he and his wife started in their home in southern California. In 1994 a book about his experience with Saddleback Church was released, *The Purpose Driven Church*. Pastors and church leaders all over the nation were reading *The Purpose Driven Church* and flocking to his conferences.

Though Warren repeatedly advised to use the principles, not the model, of Saddleback, many pastors attempted to bring the model back to their churches. Hawaiian shirts and flip-flops do not work in a church in Cincinnati, Ohio, in January, but some tried. People were grasping for that one great fix, and it was not a Hawaiian shirt. Church leaders were not willing to put in the time and labor as did Rick Warren and his wife for many years, allowing the Holy Spirit to grow the church and all its people, including the pastor and other leaders.

Many churches in phase 4 of decline believe they cannot afford the time to rebuild the church upon solid principle-based labor for the Lord. For a few at the end of phase 4 and entering phase 5, this might be true, but most can be reversed. However, grasping for straws is not the answer. Jim Collins refers to this as grasping for a savior.[6] The church already has a savior. We do not need another one. What we need is to follow His commission to the Church, the Great Commission. "*Go, therefore, and make disciples of all nations, baptizing them in the name of the Father and of the Son and of the Holy Spirit, teaching them to observe everything I have commanded you. And remember, I am with you always, to the end of the age*" (Matthew 28:19–20).

I was speaking with a pastor of a small church in a small agricultural town several years ago. His church had been in existence for a little more than fifty years and was part of a traditional mainline denomination. I had visited the church and knew it was a very traditional church. The pastor had been at the church for four or five years at the time and wanted to see the church grow. He had been to a conference on small groups and decided this was what his church needed for future growth. He went back to his church, talked to his leaders, and formed a committee to lead the church to move away from its traditional roots of Sunday school and implement a small-group concept for the church. Less than a year later, the pastor left that church—by request of the church.

Does this mean small groups are bad and Sunday school is good? No, not by any stretch of the imagination. Small groups work great in some churches. At the time of our conversation when the pastor stated he was going to lead the church to small groups instead of Sunday school, I actually cautioned him about his approach in moving the church in this direction, because of the age of the church and his proposed short timeline. The dilemma in this scenario was not with the "what" but with "how." This ordeal that led to the pastor's dismissal was not necessarily about small groups. It was about the approach used to attempt to "change" the church.

This was, in the pastor's eyes, the latest and greatest discovery that would turn the church around. The pastor did not count the consequences. Instead of looking at the history and all the factors involved, he was willing to throw the traditional institution of Sunday school overboard for this new "savior," small groups. This was the latest in a series of this pastor's latest, greatest findings of innovations. And it would be the one that cost the pastor his position at the church.

I was recently called to speak with the leaders of a church to possibly assist the church in a transition after the recent retirement of the senior pastor. Meeting with this group of leaders for about an hour, it was apparent to me that this church had been making a series of injurious decisions for several years. The detriment of decisions is not always visible to those making the decisions. However, just as success comes from making one good decision after another, a series of bad decisions will lead a church through the phases of decline at an accelerated rate.

This church had been in existence less than seven years and found itself already in phase 4 decline. In their own words, one major decision the church had made within the previous twelve months was made on the presumption of it being the "savior" decision for the church. It was an act of desperation. The expectations were built on a model and a hopeful desperation grasp to keep the church from falling into phase 5.

We do not need to grasp for the latest and greatest technique or program. To dig out of phase 4 of decline, we do not need the newest methods. What is needed is to follow a methodical process that leads the church back to its first love and reaching people for Christ.

Implementing the concepts in section 2 of this book will assist you in developing a methodical course of action that is right for your church. Considering and implementing the concepts is only the beginning. Church leaders and the church as a body must be committed to following the designed course of action to effectively reverse the decline in the church. A church does not reach phase 4 in one week. Neither will it dig out in one week. Reversal comes one step, one good decision, at a time over a prolonged period of time.

5

Phase 5: Relinquishment of Ministry

Phase 5, relinquishment of ministry, is exactly that, letting go of the ministry. When a church reaches phase 5, the church is, for all practical purposes, dead, no longer able to carry out ministry.

Some churches reach this phase when they no longer have people or financial resources to maintain the facilities, much less carry out ministry. This is a sad day for the church. The one consolation is if the facilities and remaining assets of the church can be used to start another church work or given to an existing church or denominational entity in need of a facility to further God's work in the community.

One church in a western state was running about ten people on Sunday morning when I was asked to consult with them. As I recall, the youngest member was fifty-eight years old. The next youngest in the church was seventy-two. The church had an interim pastor who was a retired pastor in his late seventies. He had been the interim (temporary) pastor at this church for about seven years. He remained their interim pastor for another six years, until his health failed him and he could no longer carry out the functions of a pastor. (A thirteen-year period doesn't really fit the definition of *interim*.)

Over those six to seven years following my visit with the church, several options were discussed. One option requested by the church at the first meeting and subsequent meetings was to have a group come in and lead a Vacation Bible School for the church. The idea was the church could get prospects to follow up with—young families with children. The obvious questions were, What will you do when the outside group leaves? If families show up with young children, who will care for the children on Sunday mornings? Who will get down on the floor and play with the children on the children's level? How will you follow up? You have only four or five people who drive. Are you able to make follow-up visits in homes?

Attempts were made by denominational workers and other churches to assist this church and make recommendations that could help turn the dying church around. However, the church had waited too long before asking for assistance. The church survived for a few months after the pastor's health failed by having guest preachers on Sundays. But eventually the decision came. The resolution was made to dissolve the church as an entity.

We do not like to see a church close its doors. But if good can come from such a closing, the good news out of this church's decision was that a couple of years earlier they had opened their facilities to a small Spanish-speaking congregation. The Spanish-speaking congregation was meeting in the gymnasium and using the education space for Bible study classrooms. When the mother church dissolved, the property was given to the Spanish congregation, which was now running about 100 in attendance. The church property is sitting in a predominantly (80 plus percent) Spanish speaking community. God's work is continuing in this community, which transitioned over the years from Anglo (Caucasian, English speaking) to a predominantly Spanish-speaking culture.

God's work can continue in a community and in church facilities if a church reaches phase 5. It will oftentimes look different and perhaps have a different cultural flavor, but God's work can be carried out. It is my prayer and hope that if and when a church reaches phase 5, the church will reach out to like-minded organizations to restart God's work in the community without giving up the property and facilities. The church that had once thrived on the premises may no longer be able to exist, but God's work can carry on to the community and beyond.

As has been stated earlier, the decline in a church can be reversed through any of the first four phases. The further into decline a church stumbles, the more difficult is the challenge of reversal. But with determination and an open mind and willingness to serve God's plan, a church can reverse the decline, even in phase 4. If a true attempt at reversal is not sought or the church reaches a point where it is unable to reverse the decline, the best we can pray for is that the property and assets of the church will be turned over to a separate like-minded, God-fearing group of believers to begin a new work in the community for God's kingdom.

An elderly lady and her two adult daughters stood in the parking lot of their beloved church. They were the last three members of the church. This mother and her husband had worked and served in this church for more than fifty years and raised their two daughters here, and the daughters had served in the church since their teenage years. But today there would be no sermon, no music, no outreach to the community. The doors were locked; the church was closed.

But this elderly woman had a passion—a passion to see God's work being carried out throughout this community. So the three ladies set out on another journey. They approached denominational leaders. A young church planting pastor was called to start a new work in the community. Two years later, much of the building had been remodeled and updated. Services were held every Sunday. All through the week the sounds and actions of various ministry endeavors could be heard and seen throughout the building, and on Sunday you would find sixty to seventy-five people worshiping together. All because three women had a passion and relinquished the ministry they could no longer carry to someone who would seek a new vision for the community.

In the next section we will look at eight major categories to be utilized in avoiding and reversing decline in the church. In each of these categories, you will find ideas and strategies to assist your church in getting and staying on track for growth and expansion of God's kingdom.

Before reading the next chapters in this book, stop and take time to pray. Pray, asking God to continue to use the words and thoughts of this book to open your eyes to identify with the necessity of change and to open your heart to the obligation of the task ahead for you, your ministry, and your church.

Section Two

Reversing and Avoiding Decline

In this set of chapters, we will examine some of the crucial areas to be addressed by any church or organization desiring to reverse or avoid decline. While some may debate about the order and sequence of these principles, I believe the order in which they are written is fundamental to the degree of effectiveness within an organization.

One of the critical mistakes a church or other organization can make is for a new leader to come in the first day of his employment with a vision laid out and ready to go. A vision is something that should be a shared ideal and perception of all involved for the future of the church or other organization. Therefore, a vision should be cultivated and developed, as we will read in the fifth chapter of this section.

There are a couple of principles to at least begin before you get to the vision. Doesn't it make sense to have the right people in the right positions of leadership before you cast a vision? They will be key in leading your ministries, so it is important to know before you develop and cast the vision that you have people in place to carry the vision through.

There is one key element even before people. That element is prayer. While we did not include a chapter on prayer in this writing, prayer must be an important portion of every step and principle. Please do not underestimate the power of prayer in reversing decline in your church. I am convinced that as long as you stay prayed up and lead your congregation in prayer for the discerning of God's will, God will carry you through each one of the principles and steps needed to reverse and avoid decline in your church. After all, it is the insight and guidance of the Holy Spirit that will lead us through any and all difficult times.

Do not be disheartened when you come upon difficulties. Instead, be joyful and turn to the Lord in prayer. You will face periods of difficulty. There is not a Bible believing church in all of history that has not faced difficulty. In fact, there is not an organization on the face of the earth that has not had the distinction of coping with difficulty. The truly successful ones stood strong on their principles and beliefs during the times of difficulty and came out stronger still on the other side. Remember, it is through our times of struggle and difficulty that we grow the most. Be joyful, give thanks to the Lord, and pray for His divine guidance.

Pray each time you pick this book up to read. Pray, asking God to infuse you with the explosive power of His Holy Spirit to act upon every aspect that He lays upon you in which to lead your church, not for your sake or that of the church, but for His glory and His kingdom advancement. Pray before you read for an open mind and an open heart, open for the tugging of the Holy Spirit to shepherd and to guide you. Pray each time you close the book that you will take what you have read and learned through the Holy Spirit to enact in shepherding or assisting your church, His body of believers.

My prayer is that God will use these eight chapters to help you share your strengths and to enlighten you in how to compensate for those areas that need to be strengthened, for He has put the people around you that you need to complement you for His glory in accomplishing His work.

Let me encourage you to read each chapter in the order they are written. It could be costly to your ministry to think you do not need to read one or more of the chapters. I believe each principle in each chapter is intertwined with all the others to form the DNA needed to reverse the decline and avoid future decline. Leaving out one chapter would be like leaving out one of the main ingredients in baking a cake or heading out on a driving vacation without the keys to your car. It will be obvious at some point that you are not going to go far. May God bless you as you read each word of every chapter, allowing His Holy Spirit to engulf you for the betterment of your ministry.

6

Filling Positions With the Right People

When planning a vacation, what is the first ingredient of planning for you? Perhaps your first thoughts are of where or when you will take your vacation. For some, perhaps you thought of budget. How much am I willing to spend on a vacation? May I suggest there is one other crucial element that must be considered first? Before the when, where, how, or any other question is answered, we must first consider "who." Who will be traveling with you on your vacation? Without the "who," all other planning may be for naught.

I am a firm believer in using the same approach for ministry. Knowing who is traveling with you on your ministry journey is of primary importance. Having the right people in positions of leadership is crucial to getting started right and continuing on a quality course of ministry.

I am privileged to be able to travel for speaking engagements and consulting with churches and other religious entities. Oftentimes my travels require flying. One thing I have noticed over the years when traveling by air is that no passengers board the plane before the pilot and crew. The pilot and crew must be on board and ready before the airline will begin boarding its passengers. No matter how many passengers or who might be on the passenger list, that plane is not going anywhere without having the right person in the pilot's seat. And can you imagine the chaos if there were no flight attendants on board? "Ladies and gentlemen, we are short on flight attendants today. So we ask that if you need a snack or drink you serve yourself." That would not be a very good business proposal, would it?

The same is true with our churches and ministries within the church. We need to have the right persons in every position of leadership before we attempt to fly the plane of ministry.

Jim Collins writes in *Good to Great* about the importance of having the right people in the right seats on your bus before you take off driving the bus.[7] I agree with Jim Collins. I believe one imperative to the measure of success of any organization is having the right people in all key positions of your organization. Before you determine what you are going to do, before you determine how, you need to answer "Who?" Who do you have in the seats on your organization bus, and who do you need in those seats? The success of your organization depends on having the right people in key positions.

The right person for a particular position might not be the one with the highest qualifications or education and experience for the position. Organizations, churches, and businesses are littered with people in positions with no passion or drive for accomplishing required tasks. A person with passion will far outwork an experienced person with no passion every day of the week. Someone with passion will overcome inexperience with his or her drive to accomplish the required task. Give me a person with passion and desire over one with education any day!

Having worked in management and leadership positions in the corporate world for fourteen years and having conducted more than 5,000 employment interviews during that time, I was aware of passion, desire, and drive in people. However, after I left the corporate world and moved full-time into ministry, a friend, Terry Herald, taught me more about this feature in people. He called it capacity. People with passion and drive are people of capacity. They are willing to go the extra mile to get the job done.

Capacity

People of capacity have the gifts of competence, ability, capability, and aptitude to accomplish what they are assigned. In one church, I interviewed and hired an administrative assistant, LeeAnn. At the time LeeAnn had never worked in a church office or any office with a computer. In fact, she was in a sense intimidated at the thought of using a computer, and much of the work she would be responsible for would require the use of a desktop computer. While she had her concerns, I saw the capacity in LeeAnn to succeed and overcome her computer challenges. In the end I could not have asked for a better administrative assistant. She was a partner in ministry. Everywhere I have moved since leaving that church, I have looked for the next LeeAnn.

LeeAnn was a person of capacity. Whether it was designing and creating a spreadsheet or word processing document on the computer or planning and organizing an event, LeeAnn always carried our plans to the next level. When you have the right persons in the right positions, the ride of ministry is much easier and so much more fun.

The further an organization gets from having the right people in the right positions, the deeper the organization will plunge into decline. A correlating fact from Jim Collin's research was that the decline of companies that had once been at the top of their industry could be traced to "what" getting in front of the "who." As good people left the companies, they were replaced by others without the same fortitude and passion. What transpired in turn was that bureaucratic empowerment was put in place to get the job done. Rules and regulations were implemented to replace employees with passion. With every layer of bureaucracy more good people left, replaced by people with less passion and not as much drive for the organization's purpose, therefore requiring more bureaucracy. Can you see the downward spiral? Churches often operate under a similar pretext.

Lead Instead of Manage

People of capacity do not need someone looking over their shoulders, micromanaging their work. In fact, a person of capacity will work better with freedoms. Passion and drive, a desire to see the organization victorious, compels him in his work. Rules and regulations will only stifle progress and creativity of these people with capacity. This is why so many left the companies in decline in the Collins' study. It is why many ministers and church staff change churches frequently and one reason why burnout in volunteers is so common in the Church. The joy and excitement has been replaced with official procedures and policies.

I am not against policies and procedures in general. However, when they become a stumbling block to production and creativity, when they are put in place to replace freedom for ingenuity and self-initiative, then we have crossed the line from leading to managing, often micromanaging. In the Church, decline will set in as this takes place.

Viewing the two words *lead* and *manage* in the *Encarta Dictionary,* one of the first things that stand out to me is that the different definitions for the word *lead* all use the idea of guiding, whereas the definitions for *manage* use terminology like *control* and *to be in charge of.* To lead is to use influence and to show the way. To manage is to have power over or to restrain. And this is exactly what managing does. Managing restrains people from being their best. It prevents an employee or volunteer from reaching his or her full potential. In an organization such as a church, this is detrimental and leads to frustration, exhaustion, and decline.

A long-standing practice in many churches is to fill all empty positions, especially volunteer positions, with a warm body. Teachers and childcare givers are recruited in the hallways. Committee members are selected because they are rotating off another committee. This style of selection process is based on what, not on who. We need to look for the "who" first, people with capacity; then we can move on to filling the what.

In business and churches alike there is a saying, "If you want something done, give it to the busiest person in the organization." The people being referred to in this saying are people with capacity. I know. I have seen it in the business world and in churches. It is true across all organization lines.

In one church where I served on staff, we had a teaching opportunity for a young adult class come open. I prayed about it and began teaching the class myself until we found the right person. After a few weeks, knowing the importance of a stabilized young adult Bible study class, my senior pastor asked when I was going to fill the position. My reply was "I'm not. I'm not going to fill the position with someone just because I can get a person to say yes. We do not need to continue to fill empty positions with warm bodies. We need people with capacity, passion, and drive." Looking back now, that was a pretty bold statement to my pastor. However, I had brought a new paradigm to this church for recruiting and enlisting volunteers.

A couple of weeks later, I asked a young man to fill in for me one Sunday morning. This young man had taught in the youth Sunday school for two years and had recently quit, experiencing burnout. Prior to asking him to teach, I had invited him to sit in our adult class teachers' meetings on Wednesday evenings. He had been with us for several weeks by this time on those Wednesday evenings while we prepared for the coming Sunday's lesson. I had watched him and felt comfortable asking him to teach for me. He agreed to fill in for me for this one Sunday.

Afterwards, he came to me excited and thanked me for allowing him the opportunity. He called me the following day and offered to fill in again when I needed to be out. Well, about four weeks later, I did not need to be out of the class, but I called this young man and asked him to teach again. He accepted. The following day he called me, filled with enthusiasm, to thank me for the opportunity. Then he followed by saying, "I don't know what your plans are with the class, but if I can help out in the meantime, I will do whatever you need."

That's capacity and passion. We talked about his desire, and we prayed for the next two weeks for God's will. He accepted the teacher's position in the class, and God used him mightily. You cannot build this into people. Passion and drive like this comes from deep inside a person's being. This is capacity.

How important is filling positions with the right people? The word *important* does not even begin to signify the vital importance of having the right people in the right positions. It is essentially fundamental to the success of your organization.

Recruiting Volunteers

Having the right people in leadership positions begins with proper recruitment. Here are three tips to consider when recruiting for any leadership position:

1) Do not recruit in the hall.
2) Look for the who, people with capacity for the role needed.
3) People of capacity have the gifts of competence, ability, capability, and aptitude to accomplish what they are assigned.

Here are a few steps to follow when your organization has a position to be filled.

1. Pray for your eyes to be open to seeing as God sees so that you will realize when the Holy Spirit nudges you toward a person, not because you know the person or because he or she has accepted before, but because this person has the capacity to undertake the responsibility of the position and the spiritual warfare that may accompany accepting the responsibility.

2. Contact the person and ask for a meeting, not in the hallway, preferably in his or her home or at a restaurant for coffee. Give the prospective leader an idea of what the meeting is about, but do not go into all the details. Details are what the meeting is for.

3. Pray before the meeting. Pray for your approach and the proper wording to use during the meeting. Pray for an open heart for both you and the other person.

4. Meet. During the meeting be cordial and remember his time is valuable. It is good to begin with casual conversation and a few questions about what is going on in his life. After a few minutes of casual conversation, move into the reason for the meeting. Choose your wording carefully. Statements like "God told me you are supposed to…" will immediately kill the interview and the likelihood of receiving a positive response. It will possibly ruin any chance of you trying in the future to gain this person's assistance in other areas as well.

Instead use wording similar to "We have been praying about the right person to assist with our _____ ministry. After several weeks (or days), we believe you have the right qualities to serve in this capacity." Continue by asking, "Would you agree to pray with me about accepting this as an act of service to God for our church?" Notice I did not use the terms *position*, *job*, or *responsibility* in this initial approach. Those terms can carry a negative allusion to a burdensome task.

From this point you can begin to answer any questions the candidate might have and explain the responsibilities of the position. If he or she agrees to pray about the position, you should leave some printed information about the position and the particular ministry, perhaps a job description if one is available. If a job description is not available, then at least a printed list of duties, obligations, and expectations of the position would be appropriate.

How do you find people of capacity and determine who are the right people for positions in your church's ministry?

The single best avenue is through observation. Volunteer positions are filled with people from within the church. How they act and react in situations is a good determining factor. How do they interact with people? What do they seem to enjoy doing and talking about? A person of capacity and passion not only displays his or her qualities in the act of service, but he or she will also be good at preparation and cleanup or follow-up after the act of service.

A second avenue of determining if a person is a person of capacity is evaluation of past performance. Past performance is the best indicator of future expectations. A person can only work out of his or her knowledge base. The knowledge base can certainly be improved and expanded, but without expansion nothing more should be expected from an individual. If someone has been asked to leave his last two positions for lack of production, it is likely that this lack of production is a trait that will carry over to future positions. Likewise, if a person has excelled and led the way with great production in previous ministry positions, it is likely this is a trait of capacity and this person will bring a passion of success and productivity with him to the position.

Helping the members and leaders of your church understand God's call on their lives is very important to each member's spiritual growth and for the health of the church. There are several tools available to assist individuals in identifying and understanding self. I have used different ones, and the one I prefer is PLACE by Jay McSwain.[8] PLACE uses assessment tools to assist you with identifying five key areas of your being. Each person is unique and has a mix of these five ingredients that no other person on earth has. In fact, no person who has ever lived has the exact same mix as you. The five areas recognized in PLACE are personality, spiritual gifts, natural abilities, passion, and life experiences.

I enjoy using PLACE because it helps to identify these five areas. As you work through the assessments, PLACE also demonstrates how each area is interconnected with the others—how your personality and your spiritual gifts are complementary to each other and how they interrelate with your natural abilities and the things you love to do (passion). It is much easier to fill positions with the right people when you and your members are aware of your particular gift mixes and uniqueness of capacity.

One of the best things a church can do for reversing and avoiding decline is to develop a prayerful process for ensuring you have all positions, paid and volunteer, filled with the right people, people of capacity. Healthy, growing churches understand that waiting for the right person (of capacity) is far better than hiring or recruiting a warm body to fill a position. Having the right people in all positions is crucial to getting started right and continuing on a right and quality God-centered course.

7

A Vigorous Face-to-face Summit with Reality

One of the major ways to begin assessing the reality of your situation is to take a vigorous look at the truth. Most people do not like confrontation. However, *confronting* is a good term to use, because to reverse decline, you must be willing to meet head on the things that may be detrimental and causing decline in your church. A vigorous look at all the truth of the reality of your ministry situation will be essential in reversing or avoiding decline.

With the phrase *a vigorous face-to-face summit with reality* we are speaking of a completely open and honest assessment—a vigorous face-to-face meeting with reality as the result of an intense investigation of who we are and how we arrived where we are today. It is my belief that a church cannot conduct this assessment without the assistance of an objective experienced and qualified person from outside the church. If you are serious about turning your church around or even avoiding decline, you should seek a church consultant and coach with experience in assisting churches in growth and reversing decline. See appendix 2 for help with choosing a consultant or coach for your church. You want someone on your turnaround team who does not have the biases that you and your church members have but has a passion to see the church thrive in building God's kingdom.

In this chapter and the next one, we will look at four key factors in confronting reality in a declining situation. First we must make an open and honest assessment. One area of investigation that may yield some of the most important information for the assessment of your church is historical eras and data.

Why We Study Historical Eras and Data of the Church

It has been said that we were given the past to learn from, the present to live in, and the future to prepare for. We are not to live in the past, but we are to learn from it. It is good to be able to look at the past with an analytical eye to gain a perspective for the future.

The types of facts and features we can learn from the past in the church or other religious organizations include behavior patterns, trends, character traits, inclusion, and the true core values of the organization. Let's take a few minutes and look at each of these organizational features.

Behavior Patterns

Behavior patterns are just what the name implies. Pattern is the regular, repetitive form or order of someone or something. Behavior is the way in which we act or respond. Therefore our behavior pattern is the regular and repetitive way in which we act and respond to life's situations. Every person uses a behavior pattern to answer a question, produce an outcome, organize a confusing experience, or minimize stress in his or her life.

Just as individuals have behavior patterns, organizations do as well. In most cases an organization will take on much of the behavior pattern of the leader setting the pace for the organization. For example, if the pastor of a church is passive and non-confrontational, the church will likely reflect this behavior pattern as well. When you see a church that is actively involved in causes outside the church, you will likely find that is a behavior trait of the pastor.

Identifying possible behavior patterns of an organization is tremendously helpful in determining strategy planning approaches.

Trends

Looking at the history of an organization can bring to light evidence of trends that may have followed the organization. Trends will be evidenced in things we count, such as attendance, giving, membership, and baptisms. Trends can also be discovered in the way a church is inclined to vote on church matters or how they treat church leaders. Trends can emerge in how a church deals with political or social issues. It is interesting to identify and bring trends to a discussion of the church members or leaders, as they may never recognize the trend unless it is brought before them from a neutral outside observer.

It is important when looking at the trends of an organization to attempt to unveil any subdued or hidden causes or reasons. For instance, if a church is turning over pastors every three years, what might be the underlying reasons? It is possible that the church is using seminary students, and the students are using this church as a stepping stone. It could be that the church likes this approach because they do not have to pay a full-time salary to a long-term pastor. In other churches, it is possible that there are leadership issues among the members of the church. There could also be a number of other reasons as well. When similar actions are taken on numerous occasions, a trend is being cultivated. Some trends can be good; others may not be lending to the good health of a church.

The important part is to unearth the reasons for trends in the organization. Many church members and leaders are actively involved in the trends of the organization and may not realize the reason for the trend. Oftentimes the detriment of the trend is not realized by the church until irreplaceable damage has been done. This brings another viable reason for including an outside perspective of your historical eras and data.

Character Traits

Organizations as well as individuals have character traits in addition to behavior patterns, and an organization will in many cases take on the character traits of certain leaders within the organization. The difference between character traits and behavior patterns is that character traits taken on by the organization may not be those of "the leader," the church's senior pastor. In smaller churches, for example, the character traits may be similar to those of a certain family or two in the church. In this situation, members of a particular family (or two) have had key leadership roles in the church for a number of years, and most other members have become resigned to some of the family character traits becoming the church's as well.

Example: If an influential leading family in the church has a bias about the education level of a pastor, the church will accept and adopt this bias. I have witnessed this on both ends of the education spectrum. One church would not consider a pastor without a doctorate degree while another church felt that a pastor with a doctorate degree wasn't spiritual enough to lead their congregation. In both cases I could see where this line of thinking came from—one influential member or family. In working with some churches I have discovered that the person who set the character traits for the church was no longer alive, but the trait lived on in the church.

Not all character traits are bad, but we must be careful when our character traits run the risk of dismissing or replacing the work of the Holy Spirit within the church.

Inclusion

When looking at the aspect of inclusion I believe it is important to look at inclusion of members (long-term, new, young and elderly), attendees and guests, and the community. The term *inclusion* implies embracing and incorporating some person or people group into your actions and practices. One error within the church is that we often do not recognize the exclusion of others by the traditions of our practices.

I have known churches who would not allow a visitor to participate in church activities, events, or programs unless they knew that this person publicly proclaimed a salvation experience and was a member of a church. I have known gifted singers who were not allowed to sing in the church choir because they were not members of the church. The outcome: frustrated visitors who found another church home or quit attending church altogether. What a missed opportunity for bringing in additional servants for God's kingdom building!

On the other hand, I have worked with churches that have embraced and welcomed guests to play in their praise band or orchestra, unchurched musicians who played in other venues on Friday and Saturday evenings. The outcome: musicians hearing the Word of God and some coming to faith in Christ.

Which church do you believe Jesus would be in? I believe Jesus would be praising and worshiping with the second one. Read the Scriptures about who Jesus ate His meals with.

> *As Jesus went on from there, He saw a man named Matthew sitting at the tax office, and He said to him, "Follow Me!" So he got up and followed Him. While He was reclining at the table in the house, many tax collectors and sinners came as guests to eat with Jesus and His disciples. When the Pharisees saw this, they asked His disciples, "Why does your Teacher eat with tax collectors and sinners?" But when He heard this, He said, "Those who are well don't need a doctor, but the sick do. Go and learn what this means: I desire mercy and not sacrifice. For I didn't come to call the righteous, but sinners"* (Matthew 9:9–13).

It is interesting to note it was the religious leaders who were complaining. If we are called to live as Jesus lived (and we are), then shouldn't we learn and practice inclusion?

Core Values

All persons and all organizations have core values. Successful organizations and churches normally know their core values, have them written down, and teach them to the congregation.

Core values are those deepest inner beliefs that are manifested through our actions. Every action you take and every word you speak is based on one or more of your core values. Organizations operate out of their core values just as individuals do.

In working with churches, I often find two sets of core values: one written and one that I refer to as "wannabe" values of the church. For instance, most every evangelical church will list evangelism as one of its core values. However, when probed about how they carry out this core value and how it is exhibited through church actions, it oftentimes becomes apparent that this is a "wannabe" (want to be) core value and not a true core value being manifested.

Your actions will confirm your core values. In fact, the actions of your organization are an outward demonstration of your core values. It is important at this point to realize the difference between lip service and actions. Some church members would say, "Evangelism is certainly one of our core values; the preacher preaches on it all the time." My questions then would be "When was the last time this person and others in the church shared the gospel with an unsaved person? Are they inviting people to church worship, Bible study, and church functions on a regular basis? How often is evangelism a regular practice of the members, not the pastor only?" Handing out bottles of water may be outreach, but it is not evangelism. Evangelism is sharing the gospel of Jesus Christ verbally as well as with our actions. We must realize it is our actions and not our opinions that demonstrate our core values.

When we look at historical data, it is not for numerical information alone. The study of historical data and bygone eras assists us in becoming more effective and efficient in accomplishing the tasks God has prepared for us today and in the future. We should not be fearful of an analytical viewing of our historical data. Rather, we should embrace this viewing as a useful, discerning, and insightful instrument for strengthening our ministry and improving our relationship with God.

More Reality Factors

Aside from historical data, there are other areas to seize our attention. A church that is serious about effectively reversing decline will take an earnest interest in the community, current members, and former members.

Community Assessment

What does your community look like? Do the demographics of the community match the demographics of your congregation? In other words, are the age ranges, income levels, cultures, and people groups in your church representative of those in the community? Are the two similar? If not, are you and the church willing to change, to reach out to show the community they are welcome in God's house? The easy and quick response to this question is always yes. However, our actions speak much louder than our words. Our words come from our brain. Our actions come from the heart, the seat of our motives and emotions.

My brothers, hold your faith in our glorious Lord Jesus Christ without showing favoritism. For suppose a man comes into your meeting wearing a gold ring, dressed in fine clothes, and a poor man dressed in dirty clothes also comes in. If you look with favor on the man wearing the fine clothes so that you say, "Sit here in a good place," and yet you say to the poor man, "Stand over there," or, "Sit here on the floor by my footstool," haven't you discriminated among yourselves and become judges with evil thoughts? (James 2:1–4).

Oftentimes in the church we sing "Just as I am without one plea." But what the stranger among us hears is "Just as

75

I am, as long as I look and dress just like you." I was in a church leaders' meeting not long ago when the discussion came up about three young girls from the community who had been visiting the church for a couple of weeks. Apparently some in the church were complaining about some of the behavior of the girls. This scene plays out all too often in churches. I have found myself addressing this very issue in more than one church. Fortunately, in this church meeting, two of the nine in attendance spoke up and understood that these girls were acting out of their behavior pattern because they had never been in church before. It was not that the girls were disruptive; they just were not use to sitting and listening to someone speak for an extended period of time.

We would do well to remember that ministry can be messy, and that is okay. When we bring people in from the outside (and I believe that is what the Great Commission speaks of us doing), we must realize our church culture is not their normal experience. Newcomers to the church must be welcomed and in a loving manner brought along in understanding our culture.

A community assessment should address the needs recognized by the members of the community, not what we as church members think would be needs. Too often we tend to offer ministry to the community only in areas where we are comfortable. I am not speaking of geographic locations but areas of service such as Vacation Bible School and car washes. If you are feeding your dog and your child says she is hungry, you do not feed her dog food. No, you meet her need with the appropriate element of nutrition. Yet, with the lost community, we want to tell them what their needs are and only service those needs, when in fact those may not be needs of the community at all. Is your church meeting the element of need of the community or handing out dog food?

Exit Interviews

Another good avenue for an eye-opening face-to-face look is to conduct interviews with people who have left the church in recent months or years. Set appointments to conduct these interviews in their homes. Let the former members know you want the brutal facts. You are wanting to improve the ministry and reverse the decline in the church, and you need to know, even if you are part of the reason for their leaving. Ask probing questions concerning yourself, your leadership style, and the leadership of others in the church.

Do not be afraid to admit that you realize you are not gifted in carrying out all areas of ministry or leadership. God did not create you to be a lone ranger. You need others serving beside you who complement your areas of limitation.

Faith Levels

When evaluating our ministry, our vigorous face-to-face summit with reality, we must also take into account the faith and spiritual levels and commitment level of our current members. You can conduct surveys and polls to attempt to acquire some of this information. But the best opportunity for the bottom line truth is to gather this information through observation. What do the members do? What brings pleasure and joy to their faces? Are there health, time, or geographic limitations? Walk alongside your people. Get to know them. Share your heart one on one and with each family of your flock.

Jumping into Lake Michigan on January 1st is, I'm sure, a very cold, brutal, and painful experience. However, there are scores of people who do it every January. Willingly diving into a vigorous face-to-face summit with reality is a similar experience. You are going to get hit abruptly with the cold, hard, brutal wave of reality. But it is necessary if you truly desire to see the reverse of decline in your church.

Go ahead. Jump in. God is waiting with a warm towel to wrap around you and move with you to the next level. A vigorous face to face summit with reality will put you on the road to reaching the summit of your ministry calling.

8

Understanding the Necessity of the Situation

Realize There Is a Call for Further Development

Unearthing these realities as described in the previous chapter is only the beginning. Church leaders must recognize the need for change—change for the better—the need for improvement.

One major objective for each of us in all aspects of life is improvement. We are incessantly seeking to improve some feature or component of life, be it physical, intellectual, or spiritual. When we discover certain truths of undesirable development (such as decline in the church), we have two choices: ignore it and let things continue in the direction they are headed or seek and develop strategic plans for improvement. The first choice is like sticking our heads in the sand. The second response usually requires a change of course, and this often goes against our nature. We are creatures of habit, not of change.

Our very nature gives us an aspiration to envision a more desirable outcome. However, our mental or psychological makeup may not be prepared to take on the needed changes to reach the desired objective. When a person or organization desires to make changes to any recognized unhealthy patterns or practices, the lack of the necessary resolve to undertake the risks of the needed change may stop them from moving forward. The unhealthy pattern is in most cases better understood (by the church) than healthy behaviors, and because they have been operating out of this pattern, although it is unhealthy it may feel safer, no matter how detrimental. Their psychological security system informs them that it is safer to stay with what they know.

Remember the Israelites after Moses had led them by God's direction out of the land of Egypt where they were horribly treated and beaten as slaves.

> *They said to Moses: "Is it because there are no graves in Egypt that you took us to die in the wilderness? What have you done to us by bringing us out of Egypt? Isn't this what we told you in Egypt: Leave us alone so that we may serve the Egyptians? It would have been better for us to serve the Egyptians than to die in the wilderness"* (Exodus 14:11–12).

Even after God delivered the Israelites, this time by parting the Red Sea and allowing them to cross over on dry ground and destroying Pharaoh's army by drowning, how many more times did they pose the same complaint to Moses? While we want a better life, even a godly life, our flesh tries to convince us to stay with what we know. The unhealthy pattern is perceived as our "safe zone."

Perhaps the greatest thing you can do for your church at this point is to bring in a coach for objective assistance in making the right decisions and moving the church forward. The coaching process supports the individuals and the organization as the needed changes to produce healthy and productive behaviors are discovered, explored, and implemented.

Seeing the straightforward realities can be an eye-opening experience for individuals and the church as a whole, and this, in many cases, should be a jarring awareness. The reality of our situation in a declining church should jar us like the unexpected sound of a loud horn blowing without warning. Realizing there is a call for further development and change leads us to the next step of our vigorous face-to-face summit with reality.

Identify with the Necessity of the Situation

Seeing how things truly are in your ministry from an objective perspective can be a harsh reality check for a church. Indeed, the further a church has slumped into decline, the more harsh the reality may be. Without the realization of the brutal facts, the church may never resolve to truly attempt to reverse the trends of decline.

Common practice for most personality types is to sit back and let things turn around while we do the same things we've been doing. If you keep doing what you've been doing, you will continue to get similar results. In fact, if your church is in decline, you are receiving less and less positive results each year, and by continuing on the same path, you will see less results this year, even less next year, and less in each ensuing year, until the church has worked itself into a hole that you cannot climb out of.

When the reality of your situation is presented to and realized by the church, it is important that you identify *with* the necessity of the situation. Did you notice an emphasis on a particular word in the last sentence? If a correction is to be made, church leaders first will need to *identify with the necessity* of the situation. Identifying the situation is not where the struggle begins. Identifying the situation should bring an uncomfortable unsettling of our minds, hearts, and souls. But the battle to turn around begins only when we identify *with* the necessity of the situation.

Realizing and stating "Our church has lost 30 percent of our attending members in the last five years" is identifying the situation. Identifying *with the necessity* of the situation will burden your heart, mind, and soul, driving you to your knees in prayer for repentance and redemption from your current situation. This remorseful spirit comes not from an emergency rescue effort to save your job or even your church. It will be as a result of a broken spirit upon realizing the neglect of appropriate elements and actions to reach the community for Christ and carrying out the Great Commission.

The biblical book of Nehemiah renders a great study on the elements of this chapter. Nehemiah identified with the needs of the city of Jerusalem. He felt compassion for the people living there, for the rich heritage of the City of David (Jerusalem), and for the God he and his forefathers served.

We do well to remember we are not talking of identifying the needs; it is about identifying *with* the needs. In church life, people more often identify the perceived needs of a certain ministry than they truly identify with the needs. If Nehemiah had not identified with the needs of the city of his fathers, a city that he probably had never seen or visited, the book of Nehemiah would never have been written. Nehemiah would never have left the comforts of the king's palace. Jerusalem would have remained in ruins until God raised up another leader. Thank God for Nehemiah's heart for the things of God and for his godly character!

Nehemiah was about to take on a daunting task that was far beyond anything he had ever been part of. But he would accept the challenge without question because he was following the direction of God Almighty. When you and I follow God as Nehemiah did, we do not see a challenge before us. We see our next act of obedient service to God. And God will provide and deliver.

The need is not about what has happened or about rebuilding the past. The need is about finding your place and purpose in moving God's kingdom work forward. It is not working against the manifestation of God's direction for His Church. Nehemiah said that upon hearing the report that he wept; he identified with the need. Verse 4 of chapter 1 of the book of Nehemiah says, "*I sat down and wept. I mourned for a number of days, fasting and praying before the God of heaven.*" Nehemiah set everything else aside and contemplated the matter. He fasted—went without food—and he prayed.

It has been said that one will never rebuild until he or she comes to the point of weeping over the ruins. When Nehemiah heard the report from Jerusalem, his passion index rose. What does it take for your passion index to rise enough to have the desire to rebuild? Tragically, many of us are simply never grieved or burdened about the broken down walls and burned gates in our ministry or even in our own lives. When you read this, do you think of how long it has been since you wept and fasted over broken down walls?

Be brave. Be bold. Be broken-hearted and obedient. Serve God as He leads. He will deliver and cause the rebuilding of your church.

Take Individual Responsibility

An interesting fact about Nehemiah is that he did not pass the blame. He shouldered the blame, and he had not been in Jerusalem. It is very probable that Nehemiah was born in captivity in Babylon and very possible he had never been to Jerusalem. Even so, he felt a great burden and passion for the city of his ancestors.

Too often people want to play the blame game, never taking individual responsibility for their situation. Those who play the blame game never get the rebuilding job done. Nehemiah refused to point fingers. Instead he shouldered the responsibility. Look at verses 6 and 7 of chapter 1.

> *"Let Your eyes be open and Your ears be attentive to hear Your servant's prayer that I now pray to You day and night for Your servants, the Israelites. I confess the sins we have committed against You. Both I and my father's house have sinned. We have acted corruptly toward You and have not kept the commands, statutes, and ordinances You gave Your servant Moses."*

This behavior follows a rebuilder who has made an open and honest assessment and has identified with the needs of the looming situation. In our individual lives and in churches, people often want to blame the broken walls on other people. In churches I've noticed people often place the blame of current problems on past leaders and former members of the church. This may in part be true, but when we fail to accept responsibility we have fallen into the snare of failure. Falling into this trap keeps us from moving forward.

This point, more than any other perhaps, is what keeps men and women from being rebuilders. It is much easier to blame others for our broken down walls and burned gates than it is to make an honest assessment and move forward with what might be uncomfortable rebuilding.

Nehemiah could have blamed others, but he didn't. His goal and focus was getting the walls rebuilt. This was the matter of most importance. It was not about who did or did not do something in the past. It was not about what could've been or what once was. Nehemiah had a burden and a passion from God. And he would not be deterred. Nehemiah's focus was on getting right the task before him today so God's work would be glorified through the future.

If we are not individually convinced and convicted of the severity of the situation, we cannot commit to the restoration or turnaround of the church ministry. One must be individually committed to the necessity of the situation before he or she can be a committed team player. Nehemiah was convicted of and committed to the necessity of the situation before he left Babylon. As a church leader, you must identify with the necessity of the reality of your ministry situation to be convinced and convicted of the severity of the situation before you can be totally committed to leading your church in needed change.

Reversing decline and rebuilding will never be accomplished until individual responsibility is accepted, not only by the church leaders, but by all involved. One of the great facts revealed in the book of Nehemiah is that it only takes one person to begin the rebuilding process. In this case it was Nehemiah. In my circumstances it is me. In your life it is you. You are the only one who can start the rebuilding process.

Nehemiah was one man. But what a difference he made! He led this small remnant of Israelites to accomplish a feat that was humanly impossible. But it did not happen until one man, one rebuilder, started right:

> Nehemiah made an open and honest assessment.
> He realized there was a need for further improvement.
> He identified with the necessity of the situation.
> He took individual responsibility.

You are not Nehemiah, and you have not been called to rebuild the walls around Jerusalem. But you do have a place of purpose and a mission to lead your church, the ministry God has entrusted to you, to be the very best it can be at fulfilling its mission—the Great Commission.

9

The One Best Thing

Preaching, teaching, in other public speaking venues and in private conversations, I often ask individuals the question "If there were no obstacles or barriers in front of you, what is the one thing you would be doing for God?" If all financial and geographical barriers were removed and all other obstacles or barriers as well, what is the one thing you would be doing for God? Of course this is not to be construed as a one-time occurrence. Rather it is to say, if all barriers were removed, what is the one lifelong mission on which you would embark for God? How would you spend the rest of your life?

Your answer to this will be aligned with a passion—not just any passion, but a strong desire you have for reaching the pinnacle of satisfaction. It is my belief that the only true way to reach this pinnacle of satisfaction is through fulfilling your purpose in life, your God-given purpose. I believe every person on this earth has a God-given purpose. To fulfill your God-given purpose, you must have a personal relationship with God.

At the time of our rebirth (coming into an intimate relationship with God), God not only gives us special spiritual gifts, but I believe He also places in our hearts a special passion. It is a passion to fulfill our God-given purpose, a passion to serve Him using our gifts and talents to fulfill our purpose and reach for that pinnacle of true satisfaction. We all strive as individuals to reach that pinnacle of lasting satisfaction. And it is only found in striving to fulfill our God-given passion. *If all barriers and obstacles were removed, what is the one thing you would be doing for God?*

Does a church have a God-given purpose as well? Some would say, "Yes, it is to fulfill the Great Commission." And that is true of the Church in general. But what about each church specifically? Has God a purpose for each individual church?

I say yes, He has indeed. Just as God has created each individual with a specific purpose in life, I believe God also has a specific purpose for each church. As God desires that each person strive to be the very best at fulfilling his life's purpose, God also desires that each individual body of believers (church) strives to be the very best at fulfilling her life's purpose.

Understanding Purpose and Passion

Before you can determine the explicit purpose of your church, you must understand what purpose is. When we look in the thesaurus at the word *purpose*, we find synonyms such as *intent* and related words such as *aim*. Your purpose depicts your intent, your aim, or your objective. A purpose validates the intent, extent, and direction of the church.

What is the intent of your church? Is it to reach the community around you? Perhaps it is to send out missionaries or to take care of church members. Every church has an intent. Most churches start out with a combined intent of all three of these items listed and perhaps more. However, over time, many churches lose the outward focused intent.

It is prudent to say that if you ask church leaders or members, they will almost always state that their intent is to reach the lost community. However, in declining churches the actions of church members will demonstrate a different intent. Reaching the lost community has become only an expressed intent, not a genuine, tangible intent.

A purpose validates the intent, extent, and direction of the church. The extent of the church is the degree or level to which the church exerts energy and resources to fulfill its purpose. In declining churches we often see the majority of energy and resources being funneled into maintaining the ministries of the current church body of members, to the neglect of the community. The further a church sinks into the phases of decline, the fewer genuine ministry endeavors are provided for those outside the church. The extent of our church becomes less and less.

It is important to know the intent of your church before you attempt to move forward in reversing decline in your church. Can the intent be revolutionized? It can, if the church is willing. In a declining church this always requires change. Once you know and set the intent of the church aright (ministering to the lost community), it is important to set the bar for striving to achieve the explicit intent. *To what degree are you as a church and as a church leader willing to commit to the explicit intent of the church to fulfill the purpose of the church?*

The purpose of the church is to fulfill the Great Commission. "*Go, therefore, and make disciples of all nations, baptizing them in the name of the Father and of the Son and of the Holy Spirit, teaching them to observe everything I have commanded you. And remember, I am with you always, to the end of the age*" (Matthew 28:19–20).

Now let's move back to the original question of this chapter: "If there were no obstacles or barriers in front of you, what is the one thing you would be doing for God?" As a church you have a purpose. We have established this fact. The question now becomes, *If there were no obstacles or barriers in front of you, what is the one thing you would be doing for God to fulfill your purpose—as a church?*

Before moving on, it is time to pray again. Pray, asking God to assist you in seeing and understanding what His specific purpose for your church is and how to lead your church in discovering the uniqueness of fulfilling that purpose as a body of believers. Ask God to open your eyes, mind, and heart to receive from Him what you have as a church failed to see or believe in the past.

Capture Principles

In many churches, especially declining churches, it is often a fault to attempt to reach for what has been working in another church, usually one of the mega-churches in the nation. The thought process is, if it worked for them, surely it will work for us as well. The blunder is that we chase after models, and this is detrimental to the health of any church. It can be fatal to a church in the final phases of decline.

If you take nothing else away from this chapter, remember this: *Do not copy models. Capture principles.* The dress code of a pastor of a church in southern California should look different than the dress code of a pastor in rural Texas. It should look different because the communities and cultures are different in each location. The worship style of a church in New York reaching Jamaican Americans will be different than the worship style of a church in inner city Wisconsin. Why? The cultures to be reached are different.

If either of those styles are working and you want to know how that can be adapted to your church setting, do not copy the worship style. Research the principles behind their worship and determine how those principles can be adapted in your worship setting. If the principles are biblically based, they can be adapted and successful in your worship set. We are not speaking only of clothing or worship styles. This is true of any part of your ministry or ministry endeavors. Find the principles of effective student ministry, Bible study, or prayer ministry and capture those principles.

You might be surprised to find that some of the newest and best forward moving ministries are based on long-standing principles used throughout the ages by successful ministries. My friend Darryl Wilson uses the term "ancient-future." When you look at the principles behind many successful and thriving ministries today, you will often find that their ministries are based on principles that worked fifty, sixty, and even one hundred years ago. Methods of ministry change; principles never do.

God has given your church a passion to fulfill your purpose as a church. A purpose validates the intent, extent, and direction of the church. *How has the extent of your intent directed your church over the past ten years?*

Narrowing to One

What is the one thing you can do as a church to be the very best at fulfilling your purpose? To reverse and stave off decline, your answer to this question must be outward focused.

I believe every church should answer this question and review it every five to ten years. Perhaps even every three years would be best for your church. *What is the one thing you can do better than anyone else?* Your church does have something, one particular feature, that it can do better than anyone else.

That is correct. Your church has one certain feature or ministry that it can do better than the government, better than the school system, better than any neighborhood organization, better than any other church.

There is a line near the beginning of the movie *The Legend of Bagger Vance* in which Bagger says to the young golfer, "You've lost your swing. We've got to go find it." This is such a great picture of the Church today! Especially churches in decline. Are you willing to lead your church in finding that one feature, that one thing that you can do better than anyone else? Only then will you get your swing back.

Where to start is always a big question at this point. The following four questions will assist you in searching out the special God-given feature of your church.

1. *What are the strengths of our church?* People have strengths and weaknesses. Strengths are normally things that a person is not only good at but also enjoys participating in. Cumulatively as a church body, you also have certain strengths. Seek out those strengths. Your strengths will align with your special God-given feature that as a church you can do better than anyone.

Remember the identifying strength exercise from the introduction of this book? People of the church believing something is a strength does not make it a strength. Set some guidelines for identifying strengths.

Guidelines for identifying strengths should include outward as well as inward focal points. Example: If this is a strength, how will it help fulfill the Great Commission by bringing people to Christ and growing disciples? You might also use as your criteria the five functions of the Church: evangelism (outreach for the sake of winning souls), discipleship (growing believers into fully mature followers of Christ), fellowship (the interactive participation of believers amongst other believers outside regular scheduled church functions), ministry (living caring, compassionate lives among each other and those outside the church), and worship (individual and corporate adoration and praise of God Almighty). A study of Acts 2:41–47 will reveal each of these as functions of the New Testament Church. Some are mentioned or described more than once in these seven verses. Does each identified strength match up with one or more of these functions of the Church?

2. *What are the local needs?* Every community has needs. The Church today has become good at telling the community our perception of what they need. It is true we have what the community ultimately needs—Jesus Christ. However, the old saying "Nobody cares how much you know until they know how much you care" is ever so true in this context. If you want to know the needs of the community, go ask the people living in the community what they need. Do not assume. I have known churches that assumed they knew a need of the community and offered a ministry to meet that need, only to find it was not a need at all.

Use a simple three-to-five question survey and spend an afternoon going door to door asking for specific needs. People will talk with you today, even though many churches have bought into the concept that door to door visitation does not work. I'm here to tell you, it does work! Engage people in the community in casual conversation as you prayer-walk the streets of your community.

Until you know the needs of the community, you cannot help them or show them that you care. Until you can show them that you care, you cannot win them to Christ. If you cannot win them, you cannot disciple them.

3. *How can we utilize the strengths within our church to impact the community around our church for God?* Here is where you start putting the answers to the first two questions together.

This can be an exciting exercise. I get excited every time I assist a church through this process. It is exhilarating to personally see the connections between the strengths of the church and the needs of the community. But it is even more awe-inspiring to see the lights start to go off in the minds of the church leaders and members themselves.

When people see that there is something already in their possession—some skill, ability, or talent—that can be used to meet the needs of others, it becomes a great motivator for ministry. It is an internal motivator that comes from God, not man. When a man is willing to allow God to use him and to develop his skills to help out someone in the community, this is when that true and lasting satisfaction begins to be realized.

4. *As the needs of our community change, can we adapt, utilizing our God-given strength base?* Another test of your one special God-given feature is to answer this question. Communities change; therefore needs change. As the community changes, can your church adapt? If God has placed your church in the community where it sits, then yes, you can—if you are willing. A more appropriate question might be, can you lead your church to adapt amidst changes in the community?

It is my firm belief that God has placed in every church all that is needed to carry out the ministry for the needs of the community around it. Before your church plunges into phase 5 of decline, I pray you will right the ship and reverse the course, using the gifts and talents God has placed at your disposal.

You have what it takes. Find your one specific feature, your niche to the community; go and fulfill your purpose doing what you can do best—That One Special Thing.

10

Vision: the Compelling Image of an Achievable Future

For years we have heard of vision and having a vision for the church. People often ask, "What is your church's vision?" How do you reply when someone asks you a similar question? Can you state your church's vision? Does your church have a clear vision?

I have found that many pastors have difficulty articulating a vision for their church. Some of these same pastors defend not having a vision with a statement like "Jesus gave us the vision for the Church in the Great Commission." So, if this is true, is a vision for the church really necessary?

First let us look at what Jesus said in the Great Commission. "*Go, therefore, and make disciples of all nations, baptizing them in the name of the Father and of the Son and of the Holy Spirit, teaching them to observe everything I have commanded you. And remember, I am with you always, to the end of the age*" (Matthew 28:19–20).

What Jesus gave us is a commission; it is what we are to go and do—what we are to be doing as we go about our daily lives. A commission is an authorized assignment, a task to fulfill. A vision, on the other hand, is an idea or image of how we might best carry out an assignment in our particular setting and culture. Therefore, I believe it is important for every church and every organization to have a clear and concise vision for carrying out the Great Commission. Not only in the church, but also in businesses and other organizations, those with a clear vision are the success stories of their areas of commerce and influence.

I want to define *vision* as *the compelling image of an achievable future.* Vision is more than a dream or a wish. A vision for the Christian goes beyond a desire for the future. It is a yearning for something that captures the heart. This type of vision is so compelling that action is inevitable for individuals or the group (class, church). Action is not optional—it is anticipated. In fact, a vision is not a vision unless it leads to action. Without action, it is only a dream or a wish. A vision leads to intentional, planned, and focused action.

God's directive to us is the Great Commission (Matthew 28:19–20). We carry this out through five functions of our ministries—evangelism, discipleship, fellowship, ministry, and worship. When we have the Great Commission as our sole driving force and we work through the five functions of the church, we will see four areas of kingdom growth.

Spiritual Maturation

At the time of rebirth or spiritual salvation, we receive a complete transformation. However, at that point we also begin a lifelong process of transformation: A transformation to Christlikeness—being like Christ.

In Sunday school and other small-group Bible study classes, we study to learn the attributes and characteristics of living a Christlike life. Studying in small groups with other believers helps us in the assimilation of Christlike characteristics and assists us in processing and understanding Christian values through the support and testimony of one another. Through small groups, spiritual maturation comes to the individual and to the body as a whole.

What is your perception of your church's vision in terms of spiritual transformation for the next year and beyond? What could be evidence of spiritual growth in the lives of the people in your church?

Ministry Expansion

As we grow spiritually (both as individuals and corporately), we realize the need for ministry expansion. As we study and grow deeper in Christlike characteristics, God reveals to us missing ministry opportunities—new doors to ministry openings, things like ministering to shut-ins, more Bible study classes, better relationship-building opportunities within the church family, etc. As we grow and spiritually mature, we not only see the needs, but people have a tendency to gravitate to the ministry opportunities where they have a passion to see improvement or to assist.

What is your perception of your church's vision in terms of ministry expansion for the next year and beyond? Does the church as a whole encourage and provide opportunities for members to minister? If yes, identify at least one.

Missions Awareness

A natural and supernatural progression is that, as we grow spiritually and we are expanding our ministries, people become aware of the need to be missions oriented. Missions is ministry outside the walls and family of the church. Ministries of the church endorse and support missions through the promotion of missions giving and provide opportunities for mission involvement on one or all three levels of missions—local, national, and international.

What is your perception of your church's vision in terms of missions advancement for the next year and beyond? How do your small-group Bible study classes and other ministries currently support missions? What can you do to promote active involvement in mission-minded ministries to your church members through the various ministry avenues of your church? How will this support the vision of the church?

Numerical Growth

I believe if a church is healthy and actively pursuing the natural progression of the first three areas of results, numerical growth will be an automatic by-product. However, that does not say that we should leave it to happen automatically. Numerical growth will happen because of the 1) spiritual growth—the more I learn about and experience God's love, the more I want to tell others 2) ministry expansion—the more we have to offer, the more I realize I know people who could benefit from these opportunities, and 3) missions' awareness— as we share outside the confines of the church walls, people come to Christ through our expression of God's love.

What is your perception of your church's vision in terms of numerical growth for the next year and beyond? Do you truly expect numerical growth through your Sunday school or small-group Bible study and other ministries? Identify some numerical goals for your church and small-group Bible study classes and other ministries. What will you do to promote the achievement of these goals? How will this assist in fulfilling the vision of the church?

Vision Development

Where do you begin developing a vision for your church? I believe you must begin with prayer. Vision comes from God, and if you want to know God's vision for your church, you must spend time with Him. If possible, the pastor of your church should plan some time away from the church to be alone with God. The focus of this time alone between God and the pastor is prayer and Scripture, reading God's Word and praying for insight.

We can find in Scripture many people for whom God had a vision. His vision moved them to action that resulted in the fulfillment of God's purposes. One idea to begin this spiritual retreat for the pastor is to answer the following questions concerning some of the personalities listed here or other biblical leaders who received a specific vision from God. (Some examples: Moses, Jacob, Noah, Nehemiah, Ruth, Jesus, Paul.)

1. Identify a defining moment in the relationship with God in the life of _____, a moment that led to the knowledge and understanding of God's vision.
2. What was the vision?
3. What actions were taken to bring the vision to reality?
4. What outcomes were achieved?

For a balanced approach, one should look at several of these examples and write the answers on a separate sheet of paper for each person studied. Next, you will want to compare the notes you have taken and find similarities and differences. Read the Scriptures about these men and women again and pray, asking God to share with you the vision for your ministry as He did with these great men and women of Scripture. The outcomes and revelations from the vigorous face-to-face summit with reality should have a significant role of your prayer focus for vision as well as other items and principles discussed in earlier chapters.

Some of the questions to be asked to begin the defining process of a vision are

1. Where are we now?
2. Where does God want us to be one year from now?
3. Where does God want us to be five years from now?
4. Are you willing and able to take on the task to fulfill God's vision for the church?
5. What will be required for the church (body of believers) to accept the vision and carry it forward?

Following the pastor's two or three days alone with God for this purpose, it is a good idea to have a similar time with staff and other key leaders from the church. For this time with the staff and church leaders, the focus would be narrowed some, based on the outcomes of the pastor's time alone seeking God's vision. The staff and key leaders' retreat would then be focused on articulating the vision and beginning to develop strategies and implementation processes for delivering the vision.

Keep these five goals in mind as you plan:

Plan actions that require results.
Identify actions that need to be taken immediately.
Decide who needs to be included in planning and implementation.
Determine what resources are needed.

Develop a timeline to accomplish the work and to evaluate process and progress.

This leadership vision-planning retreat can take place at or away from the church facilities. It could be a weekend (Friday night, Saturday) or all-day Saturday retreat. It could also be a series of nightly meetings (one per week) carried out over a period of consecutive weeks.

Allow enough time in each session to accomplish a certain amount of the vision planning stages. Do not rush the process, but also do not drag it out into a several-month ordeal, as interest will wane and discouragement and boredom will set in. Set a time frame to complete the vision planning strategy.

When your vision is ready, remember to keep the vision in front of the people in various ways and formats. Provide continuous avenues and opportunities for church members and followers to live out the vision. Without action, your vision becomes only a dream. And always remember that the vision must be recast periodically (at least annually).

Keeping the vision and recasting the vision are two different elements of a successful working vision. Keeping the vision in front of the people in your church requires strategies for continued awareness of members and followers to persist in striving for accomplishment of the vision.

For example, let's say your vision includes "Sharing an awareness of the love of God with the community." You will want to keep this in front of the church

1) in print (bulletins, newsletters, posters, bulletin boards)
2) verbally (from the pulpit, in various small-group settings, e.g., Bible study classes, choirs, ministry

groups, committees, from various staff members and church leaders)

3) in media (Power Point slides, video clips of ministry in action by your members, testimonies from members and community neighbors who have been touched by the church)

4) by providing opportunities for the church to participate in carrying out the vision

Recasting

Recasting the vision involves celebrating the victories and expanding the vision. It is important to recast the vision (preferably annually) to share the victories as a church family and to elaborate on the next steps or phases of the vision and the significance of continuing in fulfilling the vision and goals of the church.

In recasting the vision, you will want to share what has been accomplished. Regardless of who or how many (or few) people have been involved, it is crucial to include the whole church body. Give glory to God for using everyone to fulfill His vision for your church. Have a time of prayer where you thank God for the fulfillment and ask God to increase the measure of service of each person in the church to continue to fulfill His vision and purpose for the church. This allows the Holy Spirit to work on those who might have been able to contribute more toward accomplishing the vision.

It is also important to expand the vision as part of the recasting process. In recasting you always want to begin with the victories and celebrate each one, small and great. Then you can move into the vision expansion.

There is no need to call it the expansion. It can simply be said,

"Because God has blessed us so greatly this past year, it is only fitting that we continue to strive in sharing with our community the love of God. And therefore this next year, we are looking forward to increasing our awareness in the community by _____ _____. This will require great effort on our part as a church family. But as God has blessed us this past year, I am convinced He will reward our efforts by providing fruit for our labor, as is written in His Scripture."

Vision is more than a dream or a wish. Vision is the compelling image of an achievable future. A vision for the Christian goes beyond a desire for the future. It is a yearning for something that captures the heart. This type of vision is so compelling that action is inevitable for individuals or the church body.

When our hearts are right, God will give us a vision that will clarify our purpose in life. Then we will become, not great men and women of God, but men and women of a great God.

11

Moving the Locomotive
(Start Slowly and Build Momentum)

Success comes by making a series of good decisions, one good decision at a time. Notice, it is not only *one* decision and not one *good* decision. It is one good decision at a time. Success comes after a progression of making one good decision following a previous good decision following other good decisions. Success rarely if ever comes from one decision. Rather, success and reversing the trend of decline will come through a series of good decisions over a period of time.

These good decisions must come as a team effort, using the information you have learned through the vigorous face-to-face summit with reality that you have conducted concerning the situation of decline in your church. "You absolutely cannot make a series of good decisions without first confronting the brutal facts."9

Though it may very well be one of the most painful aspects of reversing the decline in your church, undergoing the objective vigorous face-to-face summit with reality will be the most beneficial action for the leaders and the members in realizing the necessity for reversing declining trends in your church. In addition, the results from the vigorous summit will provide clarity to the path of redemption of the ministry to which God has called you.

Your church likely did not drop through the phases of decline overnight. Therefore it would be unfair to expect an overnight recovery. Pray for patience and a discerning mind and heart for God's will to be accomplished. Keep the thought in mind: Success comes one good decision at a time. Build one good decision upon another.

A Steam Locomotive

Perhaps you have seen video clips in movies or on television shows of a steam locomotive taking off from a depot. You hear the water boiling and see the steam rolling, and at the right time the engineer pulls a lever, and you hear that steam being transformed into energy, energy to turn the wheels on the train. It is then that you see the wheels turn slightly and ever so slowly. The engineer pulls again, the engine bellows, and the wheels turn again, slightly and slowly. Another pull, and the wheels turn a little more and slightly faster. The actions are repeated again and again. Each time the wheels move with slightly more speed than the last. All the wheels turn simultaneously, and each turn is faintly greater than the one before, each turn building momentum from the previous turn.

This process continues until the train is moving and generating speed and seemingly pulling its own weight. Momentum has kicked in, and the train will continue to move down the track, headed for its destination. The wheels are now turning with ease. The engineer's job now becomes maintaining the correct pressure on the boiler and, as needed, converting that steam into the energy needed to maintain the forward motion and speed of the train.

To reverse the decline in a church requires not one turn of the ignition but a series of good decisions, each one building upon previous decisions. Like the steam locomotive, it takes time and energy exercised in the right direction. All of the train's wheels are always pulling in the same direction. To get the train moving, each blast of energy is pushing the wheels in the same direction. Every blast is for forward motion.

As a church you must set the course (this is articulating the vision), and from that moment every decision made needs to be to move the church forward. You cannot go in different directions. The track is set, and every move will be either forward or backward. To make one not-so-good decision or the lack of a decision to move the church forward only thwarts the momentum gained by previous actions and good decisions.

To gain momentum is to make each decision with God's wisdom and with the express intention and purpose to move the church forward. Each good decision will improve the church's momentum, until the church appears to be moving on its own, as does the train. Every good, solid decision you make is fueling the locomotive of the church forward. It is helping gain the momentum to propel your church to be the church God wants it to be.

Gaining Momentum

The caution here is to remember the engineer. He did not stop or let off the lever creating forward progress. As the train moved forward, it still required energy and power to arrive at its cruising speed and to maintain that speed. In the church there are always decisions to be made. There is always forward progress required. Good decisions require a team effort. It is imperative that you strive to have and keep the right people in positions of leadership, as described in chapter 6.

Develop a process for making decisions that will positively impact the forward progress of your church. Who will be involved in the decision-making process? Who will be impacted by the decision? What could the decision impact negatively? What could the decision impact positively? How will your decision-making team come to a resolution? When will you know that the decision is the right decision at the right time? Successful leaders realize they need not "yes men" but people with freedom to think, discuss, and debate the pros and cons of each impending decision.

Prayer

In your opinion, what one important factor is critical to a church making good decisions? I believe it begins with prayer. We must always remember that prayer is the pavement for all spiritual highways.

Decision-making prayer should be a community effort. The pastor and leaders of the church must travel through a season of prayer and then lead the church through a season of prayer for each upcoming decision. Pray as you contemplate a decision. Pray before you make a decision. Pray for the decision to be made. Pray for assurance of the decision— not only your assurance but the assurance of all whom the decision will affect. Pray that the decision will be carried through. And pray for God to receive the glory for the effects and results of the decision.

Community Decision Making

In the preceding paragraph, we stated that decision-making prayer should be a community effort. Decision making also should always be a community endeavor. I do not believe God created anyone to be a lone ranger. Even the Lone Ranger had Tonto. Successful businesses, organizations, and churches rarely if ever have a "one man makes all the decisions" mentality. Wise leaders make great leaders, and great leaders realize it is not the decisions you make as a leader but the people you bring alongside you who together develop good decisions that lead to greatness and the success of the organization.

The church is no place for anarchy or monarchy. A church needs shared leadership, and a senior pastor needs to grasp this ideal and seize the opportunity to build leaders in the church. Having the right people in all positions of leadership (see chapter 6, "Filling Positions With the Right People") will help build the leadership team required for making right and good decisions to move the church forward. It also builds the community of success needed to reverse the decline in your church.

The senior pastor is ultimately responsible once a decision is agreed upon. However, by using the team consensus approach, it becomes a shared ownership and is more likely to be accepted by the church and carried through successfully.

Moving the Locomotive through Different Approaches

Unlike the train, where the engineer is primarily responsible for moving the locomotive forward, a church has different ministries. Therefore there are varying avenues in moving the church forward and creating forward momentum. The pastor should lead the effort, but ministry leaders and members share in the responsibility of forward progress of the church.

Proper equipping of the members of the church, which begins with those in leadership positions, now becomes essential. Without proper equipping of leaders, it is not so likely that all ministries will be part of the forward-momentum building process of the church.

An important decision for church leaders at this juncture is to determine how each ministry can benefit the reversal of decline and the forward-moving progress of the church. This, too, is not a decision that will automatically come to pass overnight. This will require some time, teamwork, and a lot of prayer and thought to ensure all ministries are considered equally and equitably. Each team leader must 1) buy into the process of reversing decline, 2) be willing to be properly equipped and trained, and 3) be the cheerleader, team captain, and equipper of the members of his or her ministry.

Equipping

Search out opportunities for equipping and training your leaders and church members to be most effective in their respective ministry areas. Ask other leaders in your denomination and church leaders in your own community. There is a plethora of books, video series, and magazines available for training and equipping church members in various aspects of ministry. With the Internet and social media avenues available today, the training and resourcing possibilities are almost limitless.

Find local training venues and opportunities for your members to attend. Church leaders may be able to travel for statewide and national equipping venues and conferences. Another great way to equip is to bring people into your church to train, equip, and resource your members. It will be well worth the cost.

Many churches lack the vision to see the benefit of bringing in good quality speakers and trainers for their members. Therefore they do not want to spend the church's finances on bringing someone in. However, if you bring in good quality trainers and practitioners, you are showing your members that you are serious and that you care because you want each member to be the best and most effective servant he or she can be. Not only will you have well trained servant-leaders, but you also receive motivated members, motivated beyond what you could achieve on your own. Investing some of God's resources into your greatest resource for Him (people) will pay dividends far beyond your financial outlay.

A word of caution: you will want to conduct some research for what is best for your congregation. Ask denomination leaders or consultants and coaches, read reviews, and seek out churches that have used particular materials or trainers. Simply because a resource has a catchy title, an author you think you have heard of, or a flashy cover does not ensure it is a great product for the equipping that your church needs.

This is another place to note you want training based on principles, not necessarily on models. While it is noteworthy to know how other churches are carrying out ministry, copying the model is not the best practice for reversing decline in your particular setting.

As the church begins to accept the vision and purpose, the locomotive will begin to move forward. It will start slowly. As you work to engage the various ministries of the church, more fuel is being added to power the forward progress. The more involvement from the various ministries and members of the church, the more momentum will be gained. With each added factor of momentum, the power source is enlarged, resulting in a shared effort of reversing decline and forward progress for the church. The greater the power source (the more people involved), the less individual exertion is needed. With everyone pulling together in the same direction, the easier the pull factor becomes for each individual.

Capture the insight of the importance of seizing God's specific vision for your church.

12

Organized Open Small-Group Bible Studies

Thus far every chapter in this section has been based on a principle or a set of principles. In this chapter, I want to touch on what I believe to be the foundation for every healthy, growing congregation.

There is not enough space in these pages to give anything except a snapshot of this principle foundation of a healthy, growing church. Much has been written about this subject, and there is a plethora of resources to assist you in designing and developing the very best organized open small-group Bible study ministry for your church. For many churches this concept has been known for over 230-plus years as Sunday school. In recent years other names have been added to this ministry concept. It does not matter what you call it (Sunday school, small groups, Bible fellowship, etc.), and it does not matter when or where you meet. What does matter is that your church needs one. This principle foundation is offering to members and guests alike a place to study God's Word for His truths to assist each person in daily living.

There is a difference between open and closed small groups for Bible study. An open group—which is the basis for this chapter—is a group of people (preferably fifteen or fewer) gathering on a regular basis to engage in Bible study to gain a joyful and abundant life with lasting satisfaction. Small Bible study groups also assist people by providing a natural channel to build relationships with each other.

In this chapter, I will not go into the mechanics of small-group Bible study (this term is interchangeable with *Sunday school* or your preference of titles). Rather we will address various factors of two principles for developing a healthy, growing small-group Bible study organization for your church. The first is passion.

Passion

Passion for Biblical Equipping

Your church leaders must have a passion for teaching and equipping people with knowledge and wisdom of Bible truths and how the truths of Scripture apply to our lives today. Teaching in the biblical sense is more than dispensing knowledge. Teaching the way Jesus taught and the way we are instructed to teach is *the act of causing someone to learn or to accept something.* In the book *Teaching That Bears Fruit*, I referenced the definition for the word *teach* and the Greek word for teach, *didasko*. The preceding italicized phrase is the combination of the two definitions. The definition for both of these words uses the word *cause*. The definition of the word *cause* is "something that produces an effect, result, or consequence."[10]

In teaching of biblical truth, our aim is to produce life-changing results or to bring about a life-changing effect in our own lives as well as the lives of our learners. Dispensing knowledge may produce biblical trivia buffs, but it will not produce life-changing learning. The Bible was not given to us for information but for transformation. We are to use our time in Bible study to produce life-changing learning in the lives of our listeners. While there is a place for individual Bible study, it cannot take the place of studying with a small group of individuals learning together. You'll learn more studying in a small group of six to twelve than you will ever learn on your own or in a larger group.

Passion for Biblical Community

Your church leaders must have a passion for community. Community is a group of people with a common background or with shared interests within society. Open small groups participating in Bible study permit people to join the group at any time without feeling lost or out of place. Thus building community among all involved in the Bible study group is imperative.

There are at least two ways to close a group. One is to study the Bible using material or curriculum with a format for sessions building upon previous sessions. It is difficult for a person to join the group after the first session as he or she will be behind in the shared learning experience. In open groups the material may be related to previous sessions but not built upon the premise of having to have studied the previous session to gain from the current study session.

The second way to close a group is to put up relational barriers. This is all too common in many existing classes in churches today. Because a group may have been together for several years, they tend to forget what it is like to be new in the group. We become so engaged in our own relationships and interactions that we neglect to truly include the newcomer or guest. This is to the detriment of newcomers becoming an active part of our small group. Though our words to the newcomer are often "We welcome you," our actions speak much louder than our words, and newcomers seldom break through to become "insiders." In case you have not noticed, outsiders do not stay around very long.

Studying together in a small group fosters relationship building and community among the participants. As we spend more time together, our friendships grow, and we bond over common issues and struggles studied in our small group. As we grow together, we spend more of our lives together. Sharing not only our stories but our time and talents as well assists in building community with those in our small group. As long as we work to keep our group open, we will not only grow in community; we will also grow our community with newcomers.

Passion for Growing People

Your church leaders and teachers must have a passion to grow people. The Great Commission says to *"make disciples... teaching them to observe everything I have commanded you"* (Matthew 28:19–20). Jesus taught us and God desires us to have a passion for people to have the abundant, joyful life that is only available through a life lived according to the truths of Scripture. Teaching should not be drudgery or a laborious chore. Teaching should be an exhilarating and electrifying experience. But as the Bible cautions, it should only be undertaken by those called of God to teach biblical truths. When you teach biblical truths and the ways of God to others, it is a thrilling and moving experience, especially when you see a truth being caught by learners.

Remember also that teaching is not dispensing knowledge. Teaching is guiding others through the learning experience. God has given us two (that I have discovered) natural learning abilities—discovery learning and imitation. As a teacher, guide people in the discovery of God's truths and principles for their lives. This is where learning takes place. Good, effective teachers do not give all the answers. They guide learners down the path of discovery learning.

As Christian believers, we are to grow people into the likeness of Jesus as we grow closer ourselves. As long as we are alive on earth, we are to be learners and to be guides and leaders of learners, always striving to observe and teach others to observe all things that God has instructed.

Passion for Prayer

As believers we should have a passion for prayer, communion with God. Communion is a spiritual union through a close relationship. How can we have a close relationship without spending time with the other person in the relationship? It would be impossible. The only way to have a close relationship is to be in frequent two-way communication with each person involved in the relationship. The more contact and open communication we have, the closer and stronger the relationship will grow. The more time we spend with God studying His Word and in prayer (communing with Him), the closer our bond and relationship will be with Him.

The closer our relationship, the more apt we will be to hear and understand the voice of God leading us through our lives. Always striving to draw closer to God in our relationship will allow us to be better equipped to lead and guide others. Through small-group Bible study we can learn with others about the closer intimacies of a relationship with God as we study and pray together.

The second principle or set of factors for a healthy growing church through small-group Bible study is through strategy: intentional strategic planning and implementation.

Being Strategic

Strategy for Equipping

The first focus for intentional strategic process is equipping. Every church needs an intentional strategy for equipping teachers and leaders and a separate intentional strategy for equipping disciples (members and regular attendees of your church). In other words, you need to be intentional about how you are going to teach your teachers to teach and a separate strategy on how your teachers are going to teach. Let's break this down.

Every church needs an intentional strategy for continual training and development of your Bible study teachers. I believe a multifaceted approach is best for our multitasking society. One of the main and most important strategies a church can employ is monthly equipping sessions. These are sessions to assist your Bible study leaders in becoming better servant-leaders, building on their skills, abilities, and spiritual gifts. These sessions should be not only for teachers but also for other leaders of your Bible study classes or groups. There certainly will be monthly meetings where you will focus on teaching skills. However, your monthly meeting topics should be planned in a manner that brings balance to a well-rounded, organized Bible study class organization. Topics from month to month should include caring ministry, structure, finding and growing leaders, enrollment (it is an open group, after all), assimilation, prospect finding, building community, mission activities, disciple building, creating new Bible study units, as well as teaching techniques and learning styles. The list could go on.

Ongoing monthly equipping meetings should become part of your church's DNA to create and maintain a healthy, growing atmosphere. I also believe church leaders should seek out, promote, and attend local training outside your church, particularly equipping opportunities by your own denomination or hosted by a reputable Christian group. Perhaps your denomination hosts statewide, regional, and national events as well. These can be very beneficial to the growth of your teachers and leaders of Bible study.

There are copious books and video resources available online and at your local Christian bookstore. Today with mass media there are online magazines, newsletters, and blogs galore. Seek out ones you find to be reputable and beneficial for your leaders. Then encourage your leaders to read and study.

I believe it is also important for a church to be intentional about how and what your teachers will teach. Most people, even gifted teachers, are not capable of coming up with their own lesson each week. And we do a disservice to them when we expect this without providing proper material. Also, when left to devise and plan our own lessons, we all will default to our favored topics and avoid those we are not comfortable with. By providing curriculum, you are utilizing the skills and talents of many people in every classroom while allowing your teachers to build and develop other areas of the class as well as to study and prepare a good lesson using the material provided. Providing curriculum allows you the comfort of knowing (for the most part) what is being taught in your Bible study small groups and that the whole counsel of God is being taught on a scheduled basis.

Devise and develop a plan for teaching. Then be intentional about implementing and upholding the plan.

Strategy for Growing People (Disciples)

What strategy does your church have for growing disciples? Unfortunately, most churches today do not have a clear-cut strategy for growing disciples. Many of these churches when asked will have a response—after thinking for a couple of minutes. However, the normal response is more of a generalized thought perception than an intentional strategy. An intentional strategy will plainly lay out the process in which a church moves an individual from nonbeliever to believer and on through various phases of a maturing disciple.

There are several models available from churches that do have an intentional process for growing people spiritually. However, remember: do not copy the model. Rather, search for the principles that make the model a success, bring the principles to your particular setting, and develop a process that works in your church culture. Copying models may bring excitement for a season, but that season will be short-lived. For a sustaining process that works, consult with others and develop a specific strategy designed for the people of your particular church and community.

How do you know if your strategy is working? You know when you see people moving through the phases of spiritual maturity. For example, you see people who only attended worship on Sunday morning begin to attend Bible study and Christian growth studies; people begin to get more involved in the ministries of the church; members begin raising questions of "Why can't we...?" for the outside community; and believers begin reproducing themselves and bringing unbelievers into the community of faith. This is when you know you have a successful working strategy.

Strategy for Building Community

Perhaps one of the greatest hinge-pins for sustaining any society, culture, or organization lies in building community. Community is much more than a "neighborhood" or group of people. Community is the kinship of similarities shared by a grouping of people. To build community with those outside the church should be a common goal of every church. However, while not intentional, oftentimes we build community inside the church at the exclusion of those in the community just beyond our walls. We must have community inside the walls to have a commonality of all things believed and practiced by the church. Therefore, building community inside the church is essential. While building and emphasizing community in the church, we must always keep before us the awareness that we are called to build community between the church and the lost world around us.

On a sheet of paper, list the ways your church intentionally attempts to build community with the world around you. Once you have completed this list, write the church's motivation for each of these intentional attempts. Now think through each one individually one more time, asking this question: What is the motive behind each of the motivators? In other words, what motives drive your motives?

The first list of motives will be the first words to roll off our tongues. "Our motive is to reach people for Christ." I would dare to say our drive behind the motive is different than our expressed motivation. As a young church our motives might have been to win the lost to Christ. However in declining churches the root of the desire is "to get more workers" or "to build our finances." If a declining church does not turn this mind-set around inside the church, it will be arduous to build community with the outside world. Therefore it will be difficult to reverse the declining trends of the church.

Strategy for Expansion

"Expansion? We cannot think about expansion right now! We are just trying to turn this church around to save it from closing its doors permanently." This is the mind-set that puts padlocks on the doors of the church—closing the church permanently. This mind-set is similar to that of waiting until you can afford to have a nice wedding before you get married or waiting until you can afford them to have children. If you wait, the likelihood is you will never have these things. You will always find a reason (excuse) to put it off. The time to begin planning for expansion is now. You cannot afford to wait until the day of need arrives.

Planning for expansion does not require finances. Planning is simply making preparations for the day when we will need for Bible study classes the extra rooms that have become storage rooms for broken furniture and props that the church has not used in a decade. Clean out those rooms now. Get ready for the guests you want and expect.

If you invite me to your house for a visit and a meal (by the way, I am available next Tuesday), you will most likely clean your house and make preparations for my visit. You will clean before my visit because you want to make the right impression. Am I correct? If someone is coming from out of town and you expect them to stay awhile, you will make appropriate preparations before they arrive.

What is different with the church? Do you expect people to come? Do you expect to have guests? If so, clean your house (God's House) in anticipation of people coming. Do not wait until they arrive. Make sure classrooms are neat, clean, clear of clutter, and updated. Prepare now for what you desire and expect one and two years from now.

Strategy for Engagement

Having the passions and strategies listed in this chapter will not bring the desired results without the involvement of everyone attending Bible study. All members and prospects of your church should be enrolled in an open small-group Bible study class, and all guests should be invited to enroll. However, enrollment is not enough. Attendance is not enough. To grow as disciples, each individual attending an open small-group Bible study must engage in the learning process. Without engagement, learning will not occur.

Part of the training for teachers must be in how to engage his or her listeners in the learning process. Not everyone in a class will verbally participate. However, you can ensure that all are engaged in the learning process. The proper use of teaching methods, good facilitation of questions, teaching for various learning styles, voice inflection, and delivery all play a role in engaging the listener in the learning process. Your church needs an intentionally implemented strategy for every attendee to be engaged in the learning experience every time a class meets. The greatest means to engage anyone is to give them an area of responsibility, personal involvement in the group. For more on intentional strategy for small open Bible study groups see appendix 3.

Passion and Strategy for Celebratory Atmosphere

Thus far in this chapter, we have looked at passions and intentional strategies for open small-group Bible studies. I believe these to be instrumental to the reversal and avoidance of decline in the church as well as maintaining a growth mind-set within the church. There is one more area I wish to consider. This one involves both passion and strategy.

Every roller coaster in an amusement park has a chain with hooks or cogs in it to pull the coaster up the first hill of the ride. Unseen by the patrons, each cog lifts the coaster a little farther up the hill while keeping the coaster on track until it reaches the top of the hill. Once the last car of the coaster reaches the pinnacle of that first hill, the entire coaster will soar on the momentum that was built by each of the cogs in the chain lifting one at a time. Without the assistance of the cogs pulling the coaster up the first hill, the thrill of the ride would never be known.

As a roller coaster needs the cogs to keep pulling it forward and on track, so the church needs hooks or cogs. What are the hooks and cogs in the church? They are the celebrations. Not only the big celebrations, such as church anniversaries and Easter programs, but every small and seemingly minute victory should be celebrated. Each Bible study class that reaches an attendance or enrollment goal, every mission ministry endeavor to the local community, nursing home, or around the globe—every victory should be celebrated. These are the cogs and hooks that carry you to the pinnacle of the hills and hurdles your church will face.

These victories are the momentum builders for the thrill of the ride for Christ. Celebrate them in private and in public. Build an atmosphere of passion and enthusiasm and an intentional strategy for celebrating all the victories and accomplishments of ministries of the church. The celebration itself will encourage and motivate others to get on board and join in the ride—for the joyous ride of a lifetime.

13

Stalwart and Steadfast

In all areas of life and ministry, we confront adversarial situations. As I read about and study the great heroes of faith, successful organizations, and entrepreneurs, I see a common thread. This common bond or thread as I see it is a twofold character trait. While each of these two facets are great qualities and can stand alone, together they solidify a man's temperament and resolve. These two character traits are a stalwart belief and a steadfast faith.

Standing stalwart in your beliefs and steadfast in your faith will carry a man farther than skill, ability, or fortune. Those finding themselves in an adversarial position may not be able to rely on fortune, skill, or ability. The two elements that can be relied upon are belief in a successful outcome and a faith to carry on through the difficulty.

One thought that may come to mind here is that the outcome might not be the "successful" outcome we perceive or desire. However, God's ways are much greater than our ways and His thoughts higher than ours. Therefore, it is worthy to always look at the outcome and see it from God's kingdom perspective. I venture to say we all have journeyed through certain situations with a hope for certain results.

Yet, looking back, the actual outcome turned out to be much more advantageous than our meager expectations. Be stalwart in your beliefs and steadfast in your faith.

The word *stalwart* is associated with words like *strong and dependable, resolute,* and *brave.* In fact *Webster's Dictionary* has as part of the definition "A physically and morally strong person; resolute and uncompromising." It is important to notice that these associations and definition speak to much more than only brute physical strength. It is rooted deep in the moral fiber and perhaps even rooted in the soul. Being stalwart in your beliefs is being resolute and uncompromising in what your heart knows to be right and holding to your core values, as they are the composition of your most inner belief system.

The word *steadfast* is associated with words like *unwavering commitment, loyal, dependable.* One definition says "firmly loyal or constant." Another says "firmly fixed and unwavering in purpose, loyalty, or resolve." To be steadfast in your faith is to be solidly or firmly planted, to be unwavering. This is to be so firmly grounded and planted in your faith that nothing can cause you to slip, even in the harshest of circumstances.

I think of Hudson Taylor, who spent more than forty years as a missionary in China, a man who faced many hardships, including his own physical ailments through the years and losing four of his children and his wife in death. Yet he continued on and in a time when there was no mass transit or modern communication. Even to receive a letter from home would take five to six months. Hudson Taylor had a stalwart belief and a steadfast faith.

Standing four feet three inches tall, another missionary to China during this era of the nineteenth century was Charlotte

Digges Moon, commonly referred to as Lottie. Miss Moon also faced many hardships away from family and the American culture she had grown up in. But she took on the culture of the people God had called her to serve. She continued on through hardship and pain, even dying in a foreign land. Lottie Moon was short in stature, but she stands among the giants in having a stalwart belief and a steadfast faith.

We could go on and on with missionaries and others, like Stanley Livingstone and former prisoners of war. If you have talked with or even watched the life of a former POW, you will see and hear from the very way he or she lives the stalwart belief system and steadfast faith they carry.

One of the great men of faith from the first century is the apostle Paul. Reading some of the words of the apostle Paul from the New Testament gives us insight into a man who was both stalwart in belief and steadfast in his faith.

> *Five times I received from the Jews 40 lashes minus one. Three times I was beaten with rods. Once I was stoned. Three times I was shipwrecked. I have spent a night and a day in the depths of the sea. On frequent journeys, [I faced] dangers from rivers, dangers from robbers, dangers from my own people, dangers from the Gentiles, dangers in the city, dangers in the open country, dangers on the sea, and dangers among false brothers; labor and hardship, many sleepless nights, hunger and thirst, often without food, cold, and lacking clothing. Not to mention other things, there is the daily pressure on me: my care for all the churches* (2 Corinthians 11:24–28).

The apostle Paul suffered all these things, yet he always had words to share of his love and devotion to the God he served. Paul was stalwart in his journey, always pressing on, no matter what hardships he faced. He never stopped, suffering through all these things. Even after all this torture, pain, and hardship, Paul was found singing and praising God in prison, witnessing to the guards and writing letters of encouragement and training to the churches he had helped to start. He didn't complain. Instead, in his own words Paul said, "*I press on*" (Philippians 3:14 NIV). Paul was stalwart in his belief and steadfast in his faith, never wavering.

God has promised He will never leave nor forsake you. He is with you every day, all day. Jesus, in the last words of the Great Commission, said, "*I am with you always, even unto the end of the world*" (KJV). You have what it takes to build a stalwart belief and steadfast faith. Stand on the shoulders of those who have gone before so that you will be strengthened for the victory and your shoulders will be broadened for those who come after you.

This is living the life of a faithful fruit-bearing servant. Holding onto a stalwart belief and a steadfast faith you can reach the summit of God's call on your life and ministry.

Appendix 1
Evaluating Ministries

It is my belief that every ministry in every church should be evaluated for effectiveness at least annually. If we are spending time and resources on ineffective ministries, are we being the best stewards of all that God has entrusted to us? I believe we all agree that life is busy and certainly too short to spend time on ineffective efforts.

Evaluation of ministries does not necessarily mean we will discard every ineffective ministry discovered. Many ministries may only need retuning, as any automobile or other gas powered engine needs a tune-up from time to time. My suggestion is that the church staff and ministry leaders set aside time each year to evaluate the effectiveness of each ministry in the church. Keep in mind that each person in attendance will have biases toward his or her favorite ministries and passions.

Here are some questions that can lead to healthy discussion concerning current ministries in your church.

1. What is the name and intent of the ministry?
2. Is this congruent with the original purpose and intent of the ministry?
3. Of the three areas of the Great Commission, which is this ministry fulfilling?

- Making disciples
- Baptizing
- Teaching them to observe all things Jesus commanded

4. Of the five functions of the church, which best describes the intent and outcomes of this ministry?
- Evangelism (outreach to bring people into relationship with God)
- Discipleship (leading people to live more Christlike, denying self)
- Fellowship (fostering relationships built on total trust and giving)
- Ministry (building a lifestyle of caring for and meeting the needs of others)
- Worship (adoration, praise, and giving back to God as He has blessed)

5. In the past year (twelve months), what Great Commission results have we realized that can be attributed to this ministry?

6. What is this ministry's greatest demand on the church?
- Financial resources
- Personnel (paid staff or volunteers)
- Facilities
- Other

7. What is the best outcome we can expect?

8. If this ministry continues on the same path as the previous year, what is the absolute worst case scenario we can envision?

9. Are we ready and willing as a church body to embrace this scenario, and can we afford to carry it through?

10. To strengthen this ministry (and perhaps in lieu of eliminating the ministry), what are some areas of improvement that could be made to return this to a more viable and spiritually fruit-bearing ministry?
- Personnel
- Leadership
- Resources
- Ministry aim and intent
- Focus (outward, certain people group, etc.)

Discussing these questions and listing the answers for all to see will assist in improving the effectiveness of the ministry and in circumventing resource-draining ministries that have outlived their effectiveness.

Appendix 2
Choosing a Consultant or Coach

There are differences between consultants and coaches. Not all consultants are coaches, and not all coaches are consultants. To boil down the main differences, use these two trains of thoughts:

- Consultant: One who gathers, reviews, and interprets data, information, and observations, which he or she uses to advise and give suggestive direction for the church.

- Coach: One who through a series of properly formulated questions guides church leaders to making well-informed decisions based on information, facts, data, and observation. Coaching questions deal with God-given resources, opportunities, and potential of the church.

The history of church consulting has been for the consultant to come into a church, spend a few days gathering information and interviewing members, write a report, and deliver his report to the leadership of the church. With this rendering of the report, the consultant's work is finished. The pastor now has the unfortunate pleasure of adding this to his already full plate of ministry demands on his time. In many cases this report gets placed on a shelf with the pastor's intent to get around to it—in time.

It is my belief that a church should seek out a consultant who is committed to seeing the planning and implementation processes through to the end with the church. Note: A consultant cannot be with the church full-time. However, a schedule can and should be established for the church and consultant to communicate regularly and meet occasionally throughout the planning and implementation process. This is where a coach comes in. A gifted coach should be well versed in assisting the church in strategy planning.

It is my belief that the most beneficial path for each church to undertake when working through the processes outlined in this book is to locate a consultant or coach who can and will commit to walk with them through each step of the process.

When seeking a church consultant or coach, church leaders should first discuss the needed experience and qualities the consultant should possess for effectiveness with your particular church. Also to be discussed is your expectations as a church, understanding these may need to be increased or decreased as you interview and select a consultant or coach for your situation.

Information you will want to know to assist you in the exploration and selection of a consultant or coach includes the following:

- Credentials: Someone calling himself a consultant does not make him a consultant. What consulting or coaching experience, training, and certification does each potential candidate have? Again, certifications are not always the "yes" answer we are looking for. What organizations recognize the certifications?

- Ministry Experience: Is it varied or very specific? Which best fits your needs? Some consultants are topnotch with certain age groups. However, they may not be ideal for an overall church consultation. Ministry experience to consider:

  - Has he worked with similar size, culture, and demographics as our church?
  - Has he worked with churches in our denomination? I recently worked with a conservative church on the brink of closing that had worked with a consultant two years prior from a much more charismatic denomination. The recommendations in his report were based on his own knowledge base through his experience in his denomination. The result had been devastating for this particular church. We all work out of our own knowledge base. Be sure that your consultant's is similar to that of your church.
  - What accomplishments in his ministry can the consultant identify as God-driven for kingdom expansion?

- Interest and Enthusiasm: Does the consultant show genuine interest in and enthusiasm for working with your church? You need at least one member of your church with the gift of discernment in the room when interviewing candidates. A human resources person or someone who has studied and understands body language can help you in discerning. Observation and listening to the words of the candidate can tell you much. Is he more concerned with telling you what he can do (or has done) than with hearing your story and asking questions pertaining to your situation?

• Character and Personality: Do the candidate's character and personality appear to be a workable match with church leaders of your congregation? The most effective church consultants are confident but humble, understanding they are not the "savior" for your church.

This is only a beginning point, an introduction to exploring the possibilities and selecting a consultant or coach to assist your church through the vigorous face-to-face summit with reality and the ensuing planning and implementation processes to a healthy and growing congregation for God.

For more information and other resources contact SonC.A.R.E. Ministries at www.soncare.net.

Appendix 3
Building an Intentional Strategy for Small Open Bible Study Groups

There are many good resources for starting, strengthening, and growing a healthy open small-group Bible study organization in your church. An effective, healthy, growing Bible study organization provides the caring structure to connect people through fostering relationships for everyone, guest and member alike, of all ages with their peers.

A plethora of information has been written about the following five elements for developing a healthy, growing, reaching organization through open group Bible study. Whether you use Sunday school, small groups, cell groups or any similar ministry endeavor, it is widely agreed upon that these five are essential.

Arthur Flake stated these in his book *Building a Standard Sunday School*. These have become known as Flake's Formula. His formula consisted of five points: know the possibilities, expand the organization, provide the space, train the leaders, go after the people.

Harry Piland focused on nine basics of Sunday school work: make a commitment to reach people; identify and enroll people; start new classes, departments, and Sunday schools; enlist workers; train workers; provide space, equipment and materials; teach the Bible to win the lost and develop the saved; conduct weekly workers' meetings; conduct weekly evangelistic and ministry visitation.

Here are the five elements of Flake's Formula.

1. Know the Possibilities: Why are we here? Why do we do Sunday school? What is our potential as a church and as a Bible study ministry? These are questions every pastor, minister of education, Sunday school director, literally every Christian should ask about his or her church. To know and understand the possibilities and potential, one must first understand why we do what we do. What is our purpose for existence? Further, we need to know what we are capable of through Jesus Christ and the Holy Spirit.

2. Expand the Organization: It is a well proven fact that a growing Sunday school is one that plans for future expansion. An intentional process for creating new units and departments is essential for a healthy, growing Sunday school. There is a lot of detail and planning involved in having such an intentional organization. Being intentional about growing your Sunday school includes knowing your current leadership, having in place a training process for new and future leaders, knowing your space allocations, and foreseeing future space needs. It also includes training your people to anticipate and accept growth and the factors that come along with growth. Expanding the organization is not something one person sits in a room and decides to do, making all of the plans by himself. Everyone in a Sunday school must be apprised of the "how to's" and the reasons why expansion is necessary for a healthy, growing Sunday school.

3. Provide the Space: Proper planning for expansion of the Sunday school includes forethought into where we will house the classes we are looking to start. Providing the space necessary cannot be an afterthought. Proper planning will ensure that a classroom is selected and available long before a new class is ready to be birthed. "For which age groups do we need to anticipate and leverage growth?" "What part of our facility would be most beneficial for this age group and most effective for our entire Sunday school?"

4. Train the Leaders: This is another area most churches fall short in. All churches need an ongoing training process for new and current leaders. In the book *Teaching That Bears Fruit*, I wrote about Woodrow and Geneva Wall. During my tenure at FBC, Mr. and Mrs. Wall attended almost every training event FBC hosted or encouraged them to attend (approximately forty-eight). The training was only missed because of severe illness and once for vacation. The significance of this couple: Woodrow was eighty-two years young when I left Ohio.

5. Go After the People: Every church must have an intentional plan for outreach, and it must be tied to the Sunday school. Sunday school is the church organized, and it is to be the evangelistic arm of the church. God has created within each one of us a desire to have relationship with other people. Relationships are built and nurtured through small groups. The Sunday school must be tied to the outreach process of the church to give those persons reached by the church a place to belong, a place to begin to build relationships. Outreach and inreach for the Sunday school is imperative for sustaining healthy relationships and a growing organization.

Notes

[1] *Comeback Churches*, Broadman & Holman pg. 19, 25.

[2] Jim Collins, *How the Mighty Fall* (JimCollins, 2009), 48,49.

[3] George Bullard, "The Life Cycle and Stages of Congregational Development," http://sed-efca.org/wp-content/uploads/2008/08/stages_of_church_life_bullard.pdf.

[4] Collins, *How The Mighty Fall*, 81.

[5] Ed Stetzer and Thom Rainer, *Transformational Church: Creating a New Scorecard for Congregations* (Nashville, TN: Broadman & Holman, 2010), 23.

[6] Collins, *How The Mighty Fall*, 83.

[7] Jim Collins, *Good to Great* (New York, NY: HarperCollins, 2001).

[8] Jay McSwain, PLACE Ministries, PLACE ministries.org.

[9] Collins, *Good to Great*, 70.

[10] George Yates, *Teaching That Bears Fruit* (Belleville, ON: Guardian Books, 2001), 18.

More resources from *George L. Yates* available through SonC.A.R.E. Ministries

Teaching That Bears Fruit

Teaching the way Jesus taught. Reading this book will revolutionize the learning experience for you and those you teach.

Teaching today requires more than dispensing information. Successful teaching requires employing the teaching methods of Jesus. His teaching methods might be considered unconventional today, yet He turned the world upside down with teaching methods that are as effective today as they were 2,000 years ago.

Sunday School Leader Equipping Sessions

A series of equipping sessions for those who lead small-group Bible study groups.

Each session includes: 1) A leaders' guide with step by step instructions on preparing and delivering the session. 2) A participants' handout to be photocopied and used by leaders and members participating in the session. 3) A PowerPoint presentation that follows the leaders' guide and participants' handout. A complete year's worth of monthly equipping sessions for an effective, healthy and growing Bible study.

Find out more about these and other helpful resources on the Web at soncare.net.

What others are saying about
Reaching the Summit

Practical, relevant, helpful, spiritually insightful, and *encouraging* are all words that describe this book. Pastors of declining churches are often so discouraged that they experience ministry paralysis. The paralysis only feeds into the decline of their churches and more often than not persuades them that leaving is the only solution. George Yates presents a case that will encourage the pastor to stick around long enough to personally lead the church out of decline. Both pastor and church benefit from the lessons learned.

The principles and prescriptions found in this book will give hope and practical instruction to every pastor. Rather than a list of possible changes, you'll find instructions on honestly evaluating the situation as well as preparing a strategic solution to your own specific situation.

—Dr. Michael Landry
Senior Pastor, Sarasota Baptist Church
Sarasota, FL

George Yates, who taught us how to practice teaching that would bear fruit, has now given us a book that will help turn the declining church around. With 80 percent of evangelical churches plateaued or declining, this is a much needed work.

—Ken Hemphill
Director, Center for Church Planting and Revitalization
North Greenville University

George Yates has a passion to see churches grow. His new book is a must read for all those who are burdened by the decline in attendance and effectiveness of the American church. You will discover practical insights into not only why a church begins to decline but also the factors that will reverse that slide and lead the church back to health and kingdom growth.

This helpful book represents years of consulting experience by a seasoned practitioner who has been in the trenches. I highly recommend this book in order to help you and your church catch a new vision for reaching people and making a difference in your community.

—Mike James
South Central Strategist/Discipleship/Assimilation Coordinator
Kentucky Baptist Convention

George has hit a home run with this excellent book that deals with a problem that every church has or will encounter. His explanation of what causes the decline is right on with what I have observed in working with hundreds of churches through the years. His simple, helpful tips to turning the church around are workable in any size church.

Unfortunately, in the world today more churches are declining or plateaued than are growing and vibrant. If the leaders of a church would take this simple little book and apply the principles found in it, they could see some fantastic growth take place in the future. Thanks, George, for reminding us of those basics that have worked so well through the years.

—Larry Vowell
Collin Baptist Association
McKinney, Texas

Is your church truly healthy, or would an honest assessment reveal otherwise? Many pastors and leaders, believing their churches to be healthy, should read this book as a guide for honestly assessing current reality. George Yates, the author, clearly and practically identifies the phases of church decline and presents them in such a fashion that they can be used as evaluation inquiries for church leaders.

George also offers clear strategies for addressing critical issues that contribute to church decline, based on his years of experience serving and assisting churches coupled with his studies in church health. The readers will be challenged to examine their church in light of the biblical mandate to reach the lost and make disciples.

—Larry W. Fillingim
Director of Missions, Noonday Baptist Association
Marietta, GA